CRIME, LAW, AND SANCTIONS
Theoretical Perspectives

Volume 6
SAGE RESEARCH PROGRESS SERIES IN CRIMINOLOGY

ABOUT THIS SERIES

The SAGE RESEARCH PROGRESS SERIES IN CRIMINOLOGY is intended for those professionals and students in the fields of criminology, criminal justice, and law who are interested in the nature of current research in their fields. Each volume in the series—four to six new titles will be published in each calendar year—focuses on a theme of current and enduring concern; and each volume contains a selection of previously unpublished essays . . . drawing upon presentations made at the previous year's Annual Meeting of the American Society of Criminology.

Now in its second year, the series continues with five new volumes, composed of papers presented at the 29th Annual Meeting of the American Society of Criminology held in Atlanta, Georgia on November 16-20, 1977. The volumes in this second year of publication include:

- *Violent Crime: Historical and Contemporary Issues*
  edited by James A. Inciardi and Anne E. Pottieger
- *Law and Sanctions: Theoretical Perspectives*
  edited by Marvin D. Krohn and Ronald L. Akers
- *The Evolution of Criminal Justice: A Guide for Practical Criminologists*
  edited by John P. Conrad
- *Quantitative Studies in Criminology*
  edited by Charles Wellford
- *Discretion and Control*
  edited by Margaret Evans

Previously published volumes include:

- *Theory in Criminology: Contemporary Views*
  edited by Robert F. Meier
- *Juvenile Delinquency: Little Brother Grows Up*
  edited by Theodore N. Ferdinand
- *Contemporary Corrections: Social Control and Conflict*
  edited by C. Ronald Huff
- *Criminal Justice Planning and Development*
  edited by Alvin W. Cohn

Comments and suggestions from our readers about this series are welcome.

SERIES EDITORS:

James A. Inciardi
University of Delaware

William E. Amos
U.S. Board of Parole

SAGE RESEARCH PROGRESS SERIES IN CRIMINOLOGY
VOLUME 6

CRIME, LAW, AND SANCTIONS

Theoretical Perspectives

Edited by **Marvin D. Krohn**
and **Ronald L. Akers**

Published in cooperation with the
AMERICAN SOCIETY of CRIMINOLOGY

SAGE Publications   Beverly Hills   London

For information address:

SAGE PUBLICATIONS, INC.   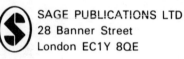   SAGE PUBLICATIONS LTD
275 South Beverly Drive   28 Banner Street
Beverly Hills, California 90212   London EC1Y 8QE

Printed in the United States of America

Library of Congress Cataloging in Publication Data
Main entry under title:

Crime, Law, and Sanctions

   (Sage research progress series in criminology; v. 6)
   Includes bibliographical references.

   1. Crime and criminals—Addresses, essays, lectures.
2. Criminal law—Addresses, essays, lectures.
I. Krohn, Marvin D. II. Akers, Ronald L. III. Series.
HV6025.C72   364'.01   78-19605
ISBN 0-8039-1144-0
ISBN 0-8039-1145-9 pbk.

FIRST PRINTING

CONTENTS

75215

Marvin D. Krohn
Ronald L. Akers
University of Iowa

INTRODUCTION

We have arranged the chapters in this book in a logical sequence, moving from general theoretical issues in the first paper, to theories of law formation in the next, to papers on the theories of criminal and delinquent behavior, and ending with two papers on legal and social sanctions. The first paper, by Ball, is a metatheoretical essay suggesting the dialectic, a broader approach than Marxism with which it is often equated, as an alternative epistemology to both classicism and positivism, the two pillars on which most criminological theorizing has rested. Whatever the epistemological assumptions, criminological theory must account for both the deviant behavior and its control which society accomplishes by defining certain acts as illegal and by sanctioning breaches of the law. The papers following the first one address theoretical issues to each of these areas, the formation of the law, criminal behavior, and sanctions.

Galliher and Pepinsky examine a number of studies on the social origins of the law and ask the question of what can be concluded about the explanation of the formation of the content of the criminal law. They find that, in fact, none of the studies of law formation in modern society has been at the core of the criminal law defining serious criminal violation—personal injury, property loss, and property damage. Each study has been on the enactment of some form or other of victimless offense statutes. The authors are able, however, to make certain inferences about the social causes of the law. Their theory is that criminal legislation is a response to anomie, and from this theory generate a number of interesting predictive hypotheses about the future direction of criminal law.

Two papers on the theory of criminal and deviant behavior are addressed to the "demise" or at least shortcomings of labeling theory. Grimes and Turk examine labeling from a conflict perspective. They propose that the impact of labeling on the deviant varies with the scale and formality of the social context (intragroup or crossgroup) in which the labeling and deviance process occurs. That process is identified as a conflict involving identification, justification, negotiation, enclosure, and disposition. Swigert and Farrel take a very different view of labeling theory. They argue that the theory has suffered empirically because the various statements of it have tended to shake it loose from its solid grounding in symbolic interactionism. While the emphasis has been on the societal reaction to deviance, labeling theory can include an emphasis on reference group identification and association, an emphasis taken from symbolic interactionism which it shares with differential association theory. This emphasis has been ignored or insufficiently developed in empirical research on the theory even though the outcome of the labeling process is clearly a function of patterns of interaction and identification with primary and other significant groups. Stating and testing labeling theory without including these very potent explanatory concepts may be the reason for the lack of empirical support for labeling theory generated by research done so far.

Thomas and Hyman integrate two theoretical perspectives, compliance and control theories, and empirically examine the ability of the resulting synthesis in predicting delinquent behavior. They find only limited support for their hypotheses, demonstrating that students who were bound to conventionality reported less involvement in delinquency than those who were not. The strength of the article and possible explanation of the weak correlations lie in its longitudinal design.

Conger presents social learning theory as a general explanation of behavior which, in spite of much discussion and critique of it as a theory of crime causation, has been subjected to very little direct empirical testing in criminology. He suggests that this empirical neglect of a powerful theory of criminal behavior stems from the shift of focus in sociology and criminology from deviant behavior to social control. Although the learning principles are themselves at a high level of abstraction they are linked fairly clearly to deviant behavior through less abstract concepts and propositions. It is a general theory which is capable of explaining both the deviant behavior and the rule-making and enforcing behavior. Conger, then, offers concepts in conflict and exchange theory which provide a bridge for exploring the application of learning theory to both deviance and control at both the individual and group levels.

With the Brantinghams' paper we move from explanations of criminal behavior in general to a model accounting for a very specific aspect of criminal behavior, namely the offender's choice of a site for committing the crime. Rejecting a simplistic environmental determinism, the Brantinghams offer a more complex probabilistic model based on Jeffrey's general "crime prevention through environmental design" (CPTED) model. The theory does not attempt to account for the etiology of criminal behavior, but starting with the assumption of some motivation to commit a crime, the theory explains why particular crimes are committed at certain times and places against certain victims and targets.

Although some of the papers presented earlier in the volume address in part the issue of societal reaction, the last two papers focus on the topic of social sanctions and their effects on offenders and behavior. The paper by Jensen and Erickson presents data on several questions concerning the perceptual or subjective aspects of sanctions. Self-reported delinquency is negatively correlated with perceived costs of apprehension, but the strongest deterrent effects are from the perceived informal costs of sanctions such as the negative reactions of significant others and jeopardizing future success goals. The last paper by Lauderdale, Grasmick, and Clark emphasizes the effects of external threats on the amount and definition of corporate crime. They present a conceptual analysis which suggests that rather than operating through a direct deterrent process, threats by control agencies to sanction corporate crime affect the amount of corporate crime by having an impact on the definition of what is corporate crime, the rate at which criminal actions are detected, and the behavior of actors in the corporate system.

Whatever one's own theoretical orientation, the reader should find these papers individually and collectively stimulating and thought-provoking. It is our belief that they present analyses and issues that are on the cutting edge of developments in current criminological theory. We are, therefore, very happy to have played the editors' role in bringing these papers to the general criminological audience. We learned from them and expect our readers to be enlightened by them as well.

We wish to thank each of the contributors to this volume, each of those who submitted a paper to us for consideration, to Dr. William Amos, president of the American Society of Criminology at the time of the very successful 1977 Atlanta meetings, to Dr. Charles Wellford, the program chairman for the 1977 meetings, and to Dr. James Inciardi, the series editor for these Sage volumes.

Richard A. Ball
West Virginia University

1

TOWARD A DIALECTICAL CRIMINOLOGY

If we return to the roots of Western philosophy in ancient Greece, we find three different paths which might have been taken by those interested in understanding the problem of crime. Two of these paths, classicism and positivism, have been followed for considerable distances. The third path, the dialectical approach, is the one I wish to explore.

The themes of classicism are clarity, parsimony, balance, and restraint. Having been eclipsed for several centuries, classicism was revived by the scholastics of the Middle Ages. The Renaissance subsequently freed thought from the divine authority of the Church, and the Enlightenment brought the Greek tradition of rationality to a high point. Classical rationalism reigned supreme, and it is not surprising that the generally acknowledged founder of the classical school of criminology, Beccaria, was a mathematician and economist (Vold, 1958:18).

Classicism is formalistic, focusing its attention upon the logic of law and the administration of justice. This one-sidedness is reflected in the narrowly intellectual view of human behavior held by the classicists, an absolutist perspective which takes certain aspects of the world for granted and tends to reify them into fixed points to which everything else can be referred. The criminal tends to be treated as an object to be fitted into the essentially a priori schema.

Positivism was also born in Greece, although it was not well nourished there. The formulation of a specifically

AUTHOR'S NOTE: This paper is a revision of one originally presented at the annual meeting of the American Society of Criminology, Atlanta, Georgia, 1977.

11

"positive philosophy" is usually traced to Comte, who developed further certain ideas of his mentor, St. Simon. Still, positivism did not really have its day until the 19th-century era of almost unbounded faith in materialism and determinism. In the 19th century, positivism became a new absolutism, with rigid rules of its own which were now to serve as the new set of fixed points to which all problems could be referred.

It was almost inevitable that the 19th century would foster a positivistic criminology, a criminology determined to be "scientific" in the sense that the term was then understood. Science meant materialism, so the new "positive school" resolved to stick to material "facts" and not to attend so much to "metaphysical" issues (i.e., basic assumptions). Science meant determinism, so the positive school would concentrate not upon the clarification and codification of law but upon the "cause" of crime. It would turn to the scientific explanation of criminal behavior, with the structure of criminal justice treated as the given. The one-sidedness of this approach is that it suffers from narrowness of scope and lack of theoretical symmetry (Taylor et al., 1973).

THE DIALECTICAL ALTERNATIVE

If we return once again to the Greeks, we discover a third possible pathway, a dialectical approach. This alternative began with Socrates, who converted the debating technique of the Sophists into something quite different. Sophistical dialectics had consisted of a somewhat cynical set of rhetorical devices which were said to guarantee that one could speak on either side of any question and win his point. Socratic dialectics was a question-and-answer method which built up a dialogue aimed at pushing the outcome to truth itself. The dialectical approach which we are examining does not involve the sophistical use of language but rather the use of language to seek the truth. This must be stressed, not only to clarify the issues we are about to explore, but also because there is a persistent tendency to backslide. If the potentials of a genuinely dialectical approach have never yet been realized, this is partly because of the tendency of dialectical thinkers to carry the approach only so far and then to lapse into mere sophistry. For that reason, we must locate the essential principles of the dialectical approach and apply them consistently instead of becoming disciples of one dialectical thinker or another. It is possible for our purposes to summarize the nature of the dialectical approach in two principles, the Principle of Expression and the Principle of Differentiation.

The Principle of Expression

Among other things, the Greeks left us with metaphysical dualism. By dividing the world into the separate realms of mind and matter, the Greeks produced idealism on the one hand and materialism on the other. Idealism is closely tied to the evolution of classicism; materialism is closely tied to the development of positivism. Both proceed by *analysis,* the division of the whole into constituent parts. The method of idealism is logical analysis of concepts. The method of materialism is causal analysis of material events.

Classical criminology is limited by the biases inherent in logical analysis. Plato had developed the idealist notion that the material world is only the shadow of eternal forms, and Aristotle undertook their classification. "Aristotelian" or "formal" logic is codified in terms of the "Law of Identity," the "Law of Contradiction," and the "Law of the Excluded Middle," three laws which provide a basis for ordering experience by *systematic categorization.* Theorists who work within this tradition tend to develop internally consistent (Law of Identity), mutually exclusive (Law of Excluded Middle) classes and to build up relatively timeless, closed, "legalistic" theoretical systems. These systems seem to exist in a world of their own, beyond the push and pull of daily events.

Hegel, the father of modern dialectical thought, spoke out forcefully against the Aristotelian method of abstract reasoning and argued for a concrete approach. He stressed *content* rather than *form,* perceiving that a priori categories developed through logical analysis alone cannot be assumed to fit material reality. In the "real world" an existing thing is never the same from one moment to the next, and a thing when situated in one context is not the same as when situated in another.

Similar problems exist with causal analysis, the underlying assumptions of which were destroyed by Hume long ago. The truth is that we do not see causes and effects at all; real relationships are too complex to single out a "cause" of an "effect." When we do this we are simply revealing our own predispositions. Others might locate the real "cause" elsewhere, perhaps in the original "cause" which produced certain effects which became "cause" of other "effects," ad infinitum.

Hegel elected to handle the problems of category and causality through the Principle of Expression, which states that aspects of a totality should be understood not as isolated "propositions" or as equally isolated "causes," but as *expressions of the whole.* One excellent example of an inadvertent yet penetrating use of the Principle of Expression in dealing with the phenomenon of crime is Bell's (1953) well-known discussion of organized crime, which has shown that this singularly American type of criminal activity cannot be traced to some specific "cause" (e.g., Sicilian immigrants), but that it is a general expression of American culture to be understood only in the context of American history.

Besides the analytical method of breaking reality into parts and abstracting from context, logical and causal analysis have in common a *linearity of reasoning.* Logical analysis moves in a unilinear fashion from its general categories (deduction). When applied to human behavior, logical analysis tends to treat social action in a Kantian manner, as if all actions were formally logical means subsumed under some categorical end. Such an approach is reflected in the classic Mertonian definition of social order in terms of institutionalized means existing in *linear continuity* with relatively stable cultural goals. The underlying linearity of this logic makes it inevitable that "social disorganization" or "anomie" will be treated as "means-ends discontinuity" (Merton, 1957).

As for causal analysis, it too takes a linear approach, but in terms of material sequences. Behavior is treated according to assumptions of completely material, linear sequences of cause-effect (S-R). Vulgar Skinnerianism offers the most obvious example. In such a unilinear model, the individual becomes a bundle of generalized conditioned responses programmed by the environment. The fact that individuals are the creators as well as the products of their environment is curiously neglected, except when some are singled out for the privilege of control.

The dialectical approach, however, does not follow a linear logic. It speaks instead of "transactions," "interactions," or "mediations." Are these ideas so far-fetched? Perhaps we might look more closely at the rapid development of victimology. In the beginning, victimology appeared to be little more than a neat trick by which the prevalent cause-effect assumptions were reversed so that the victim and not the offender became the "cause" of the offense. Since then we have seen more and more clearly that many crimes are really transactions or interactions between victim and offender in which the reciprocity is so involved that it is foolish to speak of "cause" and "effect" (Schafer, 1968). Without knowing it, victimology has built itself upon an implicitly dialectical approach. The problem is that few criminologists are sufficiently aware of their own epistemological assumptions to formulate a new approach with any consistency. This problem is compounded in the case of the dialectical approach if for no other reason than the fallacious identification of dialectics with Marxism.

Let us consider one of the perennial problems of criminology, the problem of determinism. This is an issue which has preoccupied such diverse writers as Matza (1964), who offers the concept of "drift"; Reckless (1967), who works in terms of "categoric risks"; and Schafer (1968), who develops a concept of "functional responsibility" separate from the notion of causal agency. Since the dialectical metalogic is not a linear logic, it transcends these pseudoproblems of determinism as effectively as it escapes the pseudoproblems resulting from formalism. They are seen as artifactual issues stemming from an artificially limited perspective.

Here is where many have misinterpreted Marx. The dialectical approach is actually reflected much more clearly in contemporary ecological theory, structuralism, and general systems theory than in most contemporary Marxism. The dialectical tradition rejects the metaphysical distinction which separates the realms of the ideal and the material. From the dialectical perspective these two so-called separate realms are regarded as integrated by a third—the phenomenon of *consciousness.* In a conscious creature there is always a correlation between a mode of existence and a mode of thought. One cannot, therefore, speak of a realm of "ideas" and a realm of "events" as independent worlds; nor is one realm the mere "shadow" (epiphenomenon) of the other. It follows that neither classicism nor positivism is adequate. While logical analysis is of immense value in dealing with abstract *ideas,* and causal analysis is of enormous importance in dealing with material *things,* the proper grasp of the whole in its interrelationships seems to require a different method, a dialectical approach. In his *Phenomenology of Mind,* Hegel (1967) takes an evolutionary view of human consciousness which locates it within a processual world of action. A personal *gestalt* or historical *zeitgeist* is treated neither as a formally logical system nor as a causal network, but as a phenomenon of consciousness, a symbolic totality in which the whole is something other than the sum of its parts taken analytically. This avoids the metaphysical bifurcation of the world into changeless "mind" and eternal "matter."

The distinction between an "expression" and an "effect" is crucial. Unlike the elements of logical or causal analysis, aspects of personal and sociocultural systems are not bound together by relationships of necessity. They coexist in an orderly way, but it is not a logical order or causal order, but a *symbolic* order, a matter of "style" or "spirit" of the totality. The distinctive elements in what we conceive of as a "style" are not logically entailed in one another, nor do they cause one another. Human selves and sociocultural systems are held together not by formal logic or causality alone but a harmony which is partly logical and partly causal but essentially symbolic. The theoretical problem is to find the principle of the whole, the rule by which the various aspects are arranged. This latter is the "style" or "spirit" of the whole. The method of proceeding is dialectical rather than analytical simply because the totality is not "discursive" like a formally logical argument or a set of causal relationships, but immediately and totally "presentational" as a symbolic whole (Langer, 1948).

In the light of all this, the Principle of Expression would appear to be a very useful working assumption for criminology. It protects us from metaphysical dualism and the mind-matter fallacies which have confused social thought for centuries. It works against the tendency to break up social reality into artificial bits and pieces, keeping us focused upon concrete situations rather than abstractions. It stresses the interrelatedness of things and helps us to avoid the dangers of a facile determinism. Perhaps most importantly this dialectical principle helps us to understand the reciprocal relationship between individual and society and alerts us to these aspects of reality which are uniquely human, which cannot be captured in the analytical nets of formalists or determinists.

The Principle of Differentiation

No so-called entity is likely to remain identical with itself forever; it may merge with other so-called entities or differentiate within itself, becoming something new and different. Formal logic erred in implicitly accepting the Platonic doctrine of eternal forms, a doctrine which treated material reality (e.g., an existing tree) as a mere shadow of an eternal idea (e.g., the concept of "tree"). Such an assumption led to endless arguments about the nature of eternal entities. It was considered an error to reach conclusions through observation of real, existing things, since all of them were of logical necessity only imperfect and by nature misleading reflections of the eternal ideas. If this seems strange to us today, it is because we have been reared in a different tradition, one which emphasizes observation and verification by reference to the material world. Still, we have not yet escaped the fallacies of formal, Aristotelian logic, for we continue to employ this tradition in striving for "clear and distinct" categories of crime, rigid classification of offenders, and similar applications of sacrosanct laws of identity, contradiction, and the excluded middle. Classicism is still very much with us.

Some seem to think that positivism has succeeded in escaping from all of these intellectual rigidities, but that is not so. Positivism is just as keen in its search for absolute, eternal "laws." This tradition, the one in which most "scientific" criminologists have been reared, assumes the existence of an absolute, eternal reality, but insists that it is a purely material realm which, because it exists apart from its observers, can be *positively* known through "objective" observation controlled by strategies of strict experimentation and rigid quantification (Kolakowski, 1969). Recognizing the relativity of cultural values and their threat to "objectivity," positivists have attempted a completely amoral stance, accepting only "facts" (i.e., data produced through their approved methods) as worth consideration. Only recently, however, has the tradition of the sociology of knowledge led us to perceive not only the relativity of values but the relativity of social reality itself, including so-called facts (Berger and Luckmann, 1967). We are now in a position to appreciate one of the central inconsistencies of positivistic criminology, the tendency to strain at the issue of human values while swallowing the culturally given definition of social reality itself.

Neither classicism nor positivism can handle social change. Both remain attached to static conceptions of order because both maintain a categorical approach to reality. In recent decades, however, it has been generally conceded that the older categorical approaches must give way to a processual approach. A classificatory logic of static forms must give way to probability logics which can deal with the dynamic flow of social processes. Here the dialectical Principle of Differentiation may prove of considerable help. This principle represents a clear break with the positivistic Law of Continuity, which states that changes never occur in "leaps" but develop only by infinitesimal gradations. According to the usual formulation of the Principle of Differentiation, change proceeds by *transformations,* with each series of quantitative steps at the level of apparent reality masking an accumulation of latent potentials which eventually break through in qualitative change. In politicized form this dialectical principle became a mainstay of Marxism. It can, however, be applied in more general terms, without Marxist assumptions. The theoretical problem has to do with the probabilities involved at various stages of system differentiation.

Each new level of development will be characterized by a new mode of integration. Since a variety of modes is usually possible, prediction is a difficult problem. There is no room for assumptions of "inevitability" here. An implicitly dialectical stance is reflected in Cohen's (1965:8) insistence that "human action deviant or otherwise is something that typically develops and groups in a tentative, groping, advancing, back-tracking, sounding out process." He goes on to criticize the linear model, stressing that "the dominant bias . . . has been towards formulating theory in terms of variables that describe initial states, on the one hand, and outcomes, on the other, rather than in terms of process whereby acts and complex structures of action are built, elaborated and transformed" (Cohen, 1965:9). This position is very close to an explicitly dialectical formulation. What it lacks is a clear set of epistemological principles.

Both classicists and positivists have been plagued by the problem of change. This is especially clear in the case of social disorganization theorists and functionalists. The Chicago School actually began with an organic analogy, treating relationships in a community as an equilibrium based upon a balance of cooperation and competition (Taylor et al., 1973:123-124). The cooperation was assumed to be rooted in a fundamental value consensus, with the competition conforming to certain rules which usually kept it short of a transformation into social conflict. For the functionalists, the assumption of value consensus became even more basic and the postulate of social equilibrium even more central. Both are somewhat mechanistic models.

The problem, however, is that societies are more like biological systems than mechanical systems. Machines may have "guidance systems," but they tend to operate by way of negative feedback which, as in the common example of the thermostat, triggers forces which maintain the total system within the limits of a relatively static homeostasis. If we investigate biological systems, particularly the phenomena of adaptation and evolution, we find not only negative feedback loops which operate to restore what is erroneously called the "natural order," but also *positive* feedback loops which amplify "deviant" tendencies. The "natural order," we discover, is full of "deviance" and change. Nature is an organized whole, but it is a dialectical whole rather than a mechanical whole. Natural equilibria are not described in terms of narrow homeostasis maintained by negative feedback but in terms of *homeorhesis:* a balance of negative and positive feedback which maintains a developing, dialectical equilibrium. The positive feedback provides for differentiation and growth, the negative feedback provides for sufficient integration to maintain the ongoing system even as it is altering itself. At points of transformation, entirely different systems emerge, but these are always built upon the systems which went before them. To this point, only Wilkins (1964) has provided us with much appreciation of the way in which such processes confuse the criminologist, whether classicist or positivist. Wilkins remains largely within the latter framework, but his discussion of the advantages of the strategy of "muddling through" over strictly logical or causal strategies comes very close to dialectical perspective without actually taking the final step.

THE DIALECTICS OF CULTURE AND CONSCIOUSNESS

How might a dialectical criminology apply the Principle of Expression and the Principle of Differentiation in actual practice? A dialectical criminology would define crime in terms different from the absolutist terms of classicism and positivism. The first tends to make an absolute standard of certain purely mental categories and to define crime as a departure from those categorical imperatives. The second takes "social facts" as absolute and defines crime as a departure from these material imperatives. A dialectical approach admits no imperatives; crime is defined in *relational* terms rather than in absolutist terms. Crime is defined as *a set of relationships between law and behavior*. To explain crime one must explain both the existence of the particular laws involved and the existence of the particular behavior involved. Both sides of the definition constitute the problem, but the total problem is even more complex. It is nothing less than the issue of the relationship between the so-called sides. In the dialectical view, both sides are to be examined as *mutual expressions* of a differentiating whole.

If we take a very general approach to the problem of sociocultural patterns, we find that it is possible to distinguish three fundamentally different types: integrative systems, exchange systems, and threat systems (Boulding, 1970:22-74). Each has a different system of expression, for each is a distinctive sociocultural mode. As a summary of sociohistorical differentiation, these distinctions allow us to understand capitalism, socialism, feudalism, and other empirical forms as specific combinations of more basic elements.

The *integrative* system rests essentially upon processes of identification and internalization. A powerful social bond exists among the members; their offspring take deeply into themselves the values and norms of the system. Sanctions are rarely needed, and when applied tend to be informal and relatively mild. Law is virtually nonexistent, and so, of course, is criminality.

The system based on *social exchange* is quite different; it has its own modes of expression. Here the utility factor assumes dominance as the fundamental principle of the whole. One conforms to social expectations as an advantageous bargain. The exchange system makes its appearance with an erosion of identification and internalization: the individual begins to think of himself and for himself. The work of the social contract theorists illustrates the new master criterion. The utilitarians of the classical school of criminology became more explicit as to the calculative processes involved in establishing the marginal utilities connected with social gains and losses, as, for example, in Bentham's doctrine of the "felicific calculus."

The third type of sociocultural system, the *threat system,* represents a form of social organization based on fear reinforced by force or fraud. Resting on negative sanctions rather than internalization or utility, threat systems tend to develop where the social bond is too weak to maintain an integrative system and social power is too disparate to support a viable exchange system. The tendency is to rely upon coercion.

Just as the "styles" of these three modes of sociocultural organization can be sharply distinguished, so the process of differentiation is reasonably clear. Since the beginning of the Industrial Revolution, industrialized societies have experienced a transition from integrative systems toward exchange systems. Toennies summarized the shift as a master transformation from *Gemeinschaft* to *Gesellschaft.* Maine, emphasizing the legal aspects, put the change in terms of a transition from "status" to "contract." Weber stressed the decline of "traditional" authority and the rise of "rational-legal" authority. Durkheim saw that one result was a situation of anomie, a "normlessness" resulting from superficial acceptance of a variety of vague, contradictory, and rapidly changing standards. The Marxists have shown the extent to which capitalism, allegedly the epitome of an exchange mode, could be transformed into an exploitative threat system as economic surplus and political power accumulated in one social class.

These sociocultural changes must also be considered from the point of view of the conscious subject, the individual self. This is something that Marxism has tended to ignore, with a few exceptions such as Bonger (1916), as outmoded Hegelian idealism, but it is simply the other side of the picture. While Hegel tended to neglect material factors, the later Marx tended to shy away from consideration of social psychological factors. Conceived dialectically, consciousness represents a set of processes linking organic systems to social systems. Although often thought of as an entity residing somewhere within the person, consciousness is more accurately described as a system of functions operating toward the integration of experience. Historical examination reveals that the feedback processes which sustain the self have been greatly altered over the centuries and suggests that changes in criminality are closely related to sociohistorical trends in patterns of human consciousness.

Although we must be careful not to overstate the case, the evidence appears to support the general positions of Levy-Bruhl and Durkheim which suggest that early man lived in something of a *participation mystique,* with the group being more "real" than the person, and with life dominated by *collective representations.* As "selves" became differentiated from collectivities, the basic relationship between organism and society was altered in the direction of individuality. Emerging selves gained a certain "functional autonomy" as subsystems within the collectivity. Cassirer (1955:171-173) describes the transformation as a new consciousness of "inner freedom." The new inner freedom made possible the conscious violation of norms and necessitated some organized social reaction. Where before the possibility of criminality was remote, the new pattern set the stage for conflict between individual and society and for a rising criminality potential. The development of selfhood was, on the other hand, associated with a new ethical sensitivity (Cassirer, 1955:173), and this development meant that direct power reactions were somewhat constrained by emerging ethical standards.

History has since been characterized by an ebb and flow in the balance between the thrust of individuality and the constraints of the social order. With the decline of feudalism, the discovery of the New World, the Reformation, and a host of lesser developments, individuality became gradually more widespread. So did criminality. It is likely that criminality would have become much more common than was actually the case had not the older integrative forces of family and religion combined to provide a mode of coherence for the emerging personalities and a set of rules for systematic interfacing with the new social world.

Burckhardt (1960:121), speaking of the surge of individuation during the Renaissance, writes that "there arose an *objective* treatment and consideration of the State and of all the things of this world, and at the same time the *subjective* side asserted itself with corresponding emphasis." He goes on to say, "Finally, we find in this country, where individuality of every sort attained its highest development, instances of that ideal and absolute wickedness which delights in crimes for their own sake and not as a means to an end" (Burckhardt, 1960:346).

When the experience of self becomes more real than the experience of the outside world of institutions, norms, and laws, a society is said to be "deinstitutionalized" (Gehlen, 1957). The most basic elements of social control become more and more irrelevant. The rapid changes in the external world connected with geographic mobility, increased social differentiation, and accelerating social change seem to produce a turning inward, a preoccupation with the new issues of self. The result is that the "focus of reality" shifts from the social world of institutions to the individual subjective world of internal experiences (Berger et al., 1973: 73). The system is governed by a new principle, and it expresses itself differently.

It is important to realize that the social psychological trends are manifest not only in new patterns of law violation but in the changing nature of the law. Law is rooted in an ethical tradition built on a traditional model of human nature, a model rationalized by centuries of Western thought. As Cassirer (1955) has shown, the ethics of "civilization" developed with the individuated self. We can see that the law can be traced to social circumstances characterized by interacting, individuated selves, and concepts such as private property, personal integrity, and individual freedom are expressions of such self-consciousness. These concepts made possible the transition from a social order based on expressions of kinship and territory to a social order based on expressions of exchange relations among self-conscious individuals.

What of more recent times? A few decades ago, Ploscowe (1931) developed what Vold (1958:176) has called "a carefully formulated, theoretically consistent interpretation of the significant fact that crime has probably increased throughout most of the Western world during the last one hundred and fifty years, despite the obvious and indisputable increase in the well-being of nearly everyone everywhere." At that time, Ploscowe stressed the stimulation of new needs through advertising, rising aspirations, and what is now termed "relative deprivation." But it is not simply a matter of *more;* it is a matter of *more* and *different.* Reckless (1967) has recently referred to a "new pitch" in crime and delinquency, stressing the emergence of personal aggrandizement resulting from a loss of "inner containment" related to "self factors" and a decline of "outer containment" related to "lack of belongingness" and "cohesiveness" of the social order. This too represents a movement toward a dialectical rather than a classicist or positivist approach. Whether it is accurate or not, it comes closer to a grasp of the mutuality of culture and consciousness than either of the traditional paths seems able to provide.

A dialectical approach to criminology is less comforting than classicism or positivism, but it is much more realistic. The Principle of Expression tells us that the problem of crime is a problem of the whole, reaffirming the old adage that every society gets the crime it deserves, but casting new light upon this truism. The Principle of Differentiation tells us that it is perfectly normal for societies to diversify and complexify as they develop, and that the notions of "social control" or "social defense" amount to little more than unrealistic assumptions about the possibilities of stemming the tides of history. All together, the dialectical approach can teach the criminologist some humility, the same sort of humility the biologist learns from the study of ecology or the physicist from the study of general systems theory. Surely this is a more realistic stand than either scientism or cynicism, both of which are rampant in contemporary criminology. What we now need is the further clarification of dialectical principles so that much which has been accomplished in an ad hoc manner can be formulated in more explicit and testable fashion.

REFERENCES

BELL, D. (1953). "Crime as an American way of life." Antioch Review 13:131-154.
BERGER, P.L., BERGER, B., and KELLNER, H. (1973). The homeless mind. New York: Vintage.
BERGER, P.L. and LUCKMANN, T. (1967). Social construction of reality. Garden City, N.Y.: Doubleday.
BONGER, W.A. (1916). Crime and economic conditions. Boston: Little, Brown.
BOULDING, K. (1970). A primer on social dynamics. New York: Free Press.
BURCKHARDT, J. (1960). The civilization of the renaissance in Italy. New York: Mentor.
CASSIRER, E. (1955). The philosophy of symbolic forms, vol. II, mythical thought. New Haven, Conn.: Yale University Press.
COHEN, A. (1965) "The sociology of the deviant act: anomie theory and beyond." American Sociological Review 30:5-14.
GEHLEN, A. (1957). Die Seele im technischen Zeitalter. Hamburg: Rowohlt.
HEGEL, G.W.F. (1967). The phenomenology of mind. New York: Harper & Row.
KOLAKOWSKI, L. (1969). Alienation of reason. Garden City, N.Y.: Doubleday.
LANGER, S.K. (1948). Philosophy in a new key. New York: New American Library.
MATZA, D. (1964). Delinquency and drift. New York: John Wiley.
MERTON, R.K. (1957). "Social structure and anomie." Pp. 131-160 in Robert K. Merton (ed.), Social theory and social structure, Revised edition. Glencoe, Ill.: Free Press.
PLOSCOWE, M. (1931). "Some causative factors in criminality." Pp. 5-162 in Report on the causes of crime, vol. I, part 1. Washington, D.C.: National Commission on Law Observance and Law Enforcement.
RECKLESS, W.C. (1967). The crime problem. New York: Appleton-Century-Crofts.
SCHAFER, S. (1968). The victim and his criminal. New York: Random House.
TAYLOR, J., WALTON, P., and YOUNG, J. (1973). The new criminology. London: Routledge & Kegan Paul.
VOLD, G. (1958). Theoretical Criminology. New York: Oxford University Press.
WILKINS, L. (1964). Social deviance: Social policy, action and research. London: Tavistock.

John F. Galliher
Harold E. Pepinsky
Indiana University,
Bloomington

2

A META-STUDY OF SOCIAL ORIGINS OF SUBSTANTIVE CRIMINAL LAW

What makes state authorities decide to change the law as to which acts deserve confinement or punishment? This question has intrigued a number of American scholars sufficiently to move them to do case studies of the social origins of substantive American criminal laws, and of their English antecedents.[1] A striking feature of these studies is that each has been done without regard to any of the others. Now that various studies of the social origins of substantive criminal laws have accumulated, we can see whether any general knowledge can be inferred from them. That is the object of this meta-study of social origins of substantive criminal laws.

CODING

It at first seemed obvious to us that we should categorize each study by type of social origin it reported as a prelude to looking for correlates of social origins of various kinds.

AUTHORS' NOTE: Revision of paper presented at the American Society of Criminology Meeting, Atlanta, November 1977. We especially thank participants in Indiana University Forensic Studies and Sociology colloquia for criticism, and Martha Geter and Donna Littrell for typing.

We ran into the very problem that Galliher and Walker (1977) had found in the literature on origins of the Marijuana Tax Act. For each of many of the cases of legislation, it appeared equally plausible that individuals, monolithic groups, and pluralistic forces had moved the legislators to act. Such ambiguities were clearer the larger the number of studies on the same legislation, with Prohibition and federal drug legislation heading the list.

In retrospect, the ambiguities are not very surprising. As one examines the process by which any piece of legislation is promulgated—especially major legislation—one is bound to find many people who favored the legislation and were involved in various stages of the process. The people will probably have had sometimes more, sometimes fewer, competing interests and allegiances. One knows that the legislation followed the input of each of these people. It will be obvious that some of these people were peripheral to the legislative process, but many people will remain whose influence might well have been crucial. For each of these actors, there is no way of choosing between two causal propositions: that such legislation (1) would not have occurred if s/he had been absent or (2) would have occurred notwithstanding the absence of the others. For all anyone can infer, particular individuals, monolithic groups, and pluralistic forces might as well all have been both necessary and sufficient causes of any piece of legislation.

As we searched through the studies, we found but three distinctive features of each piece of legislation that we could unambiguously categorize: (1) the substance of the legislation itself, and the (2) time and (3) place in which

---

One of our arguments was over whose name should go first, each of us pushing for the other to go ahead of himself. Our compromise is to make explicit our disclaimer: we mean to imply no seniority of authorship. The study would not have resulted but for the contributions of us both. At the same time, we have found that we disagree even on how to interpret the studies we are analyzing. Interpretation of the kind we have undertaken is inherently controversial, and the views we now publish are not necessarily those of both authors.

the process of legislation took place. This is shown in Table 1 which lists the set of studies we found prominent in sociology of criminal law literature.[2]

Table 1: Studies Surveyed

	Subject of Law	Time	Place
Jeffery (1956)	Common law of crime	400-1200	England
Chambliss (1964)	Vagrancy	1349-1743	England
Hall (1952)	Theft	1450-1950 (especially Carrier's Case, 1473, England, and court-made law of that period)	England United States
Haskins (1960)	Creation of total penal code	1630-1650	Massachusetts
Nelson (1967)	Revision of total penal code	1760-1810	Massachusetts
Gusfield (1963)	Prohibition	1826-1960	United States
Sinclair (1962)	Prohibition	1840-1933	United States
Lindesmith (1965)	Drug control	1861-1963	United States
Duster (1970)	Drug control	1865-1966	United States federal government and California
Platt (1969)	Juvenile code	1870-1900	Illinois
Timberlake (1963)	Prohibition	1900-1920	United States
Bonnie and Whitebread (1974)	Marijuana control	1900-1973	United States
Musto (1973)	Drug control	1906-1937	United States
McCaghy and Denisoff (1973)	Musical record pirating	1906-1971	United States
Dickson (1968)	Marijuana Tax Act	1914-1940s	United States
Becker (1963)	Marijuana Tax Act	1925-1937	United States
Sutherland (1950)	Sexual psychopathy	1937-1950	United States
Roby (1969)	Prostitution	1961-1967	New York
Galliher et al. (1974)	Marijuana control	1968-1969	Nebraska
Graham (1972)	Amphetamine control	1969-1970	United States

COMMONALITIES AMONG STUDIES

There are two clusters of studies in the Table of Studies Surveyed. One, concentrating on legislation accompanying the rise of commerce in the several centuries preceding the Industrial Revolution in England, consists of Chambliss's (1964) study of vagrancy statutes and Hall's (1952) study of court-made changes in the law of theft. The other is of studies of processes leading to statutory change in the United States since the end of the 19th century. Jeffrey's (1957), Haskins's (1960), and Nelson's (1967) studies each deal with legislation in a unique setting, and so belong to no cluster.

Sellin and Wolfgang's (1964) categories of crime lend themselves to classifying the legislation in each of the two clusters. Sellin and Wolfgang classify crime by three categories of harm the crimes do: personal injury (as in assault), property loss (as in theft), and damage to property (as in vandalism). Chambliss (1964) and Hall (1952) deal with redefinition of property loss crimes. Although we have grown accustomed to considering vagrancy a victimless crime in the United States in this century, Chambliss found that, in the period he studied in England, the need especially for agricultural labor was critical and vagrancy was seen as a deprivation of employers' rights to retain human labor. Vagrants were seen as stealing resources belonging to producers of goods and services. Beier (1974:26-29) confirms the idea that vagrants were persecuted in an attempt to maintain master-servant relationships in the face of growing commercialism and individualism. And in his analysis of Carrier's Case, Hall (1952) found that the common law of theft—previously suited to protecting property interests in a feudal landholding economy—had to be expanded to define property rights in mercantile exchange.

It could easily be mere coincidence that two studies of the same time and place analyzed the same category of legislation. The coincidence is far more improbable for the large number of studies of legislation in the contemporary

United States. With a single exception—in McCaghy and Denisoff (1973)—the legislation studied falls into *none* of Sellin and Wolfgang's categories, which deal with problems of imbalance in social exchange, with issues of people taking an undue measure of each other's bodies or possessions in the course of interaction. In most of the studies of contemporary American legislation, by contrast, the harm legislated against is that of treating social exchange as meaningless in a variety of ways: by altering one's state of consciousness with liquor (Gusfield, 1963; Sinclair, 1962; Timberlake, 1963) or drugs (Lindesmith, 1965; Musto, 1973; Duster, 1970; Bonnie and Whitebread, 1974; Dickson, 1968; Becker, 1963; Graham, 1972; Galliher et al., 1974); by detachment from parental control (Platt, 1969); by a failure of ego development (Sutherland, 1950); and by detaching physical from social intercourse (Roby, 1969).

SIGNIFICANCE OF THE COMMONALITIES

Could the near uniformity of legal subject matter in both clusters be accidental? If so, it is an accident of remarkable proportions. How might the uniformities be accounted for? Could it simply be that scholars have been more willing to recognize depredation as a source of legislation in other times and places than in their own? This seems not to be the case. Scholars of crime control have shown little reluctance to raise alarms over the current propensity of Americans to prey on one another. One school of thought, represented by Platt (1969) and Quinney (1970), believes that crime legislation is itself a weapon of prey: a tool for one class to use to exploit another. Interestingly, as Quinney takes pains to defend this proposition, he cites Chambliss (1964) and Hall (1952) rather than studies of contemporary American legislative definitions of crime for support. Contemporary crime legislation, like that creating the Law Enforcement Assistance Administration, is cited by Quinney (1974) and others, but this legislation is not *substantive:* it is only incidentally a vehicle for redefinition of criminal behavior.

Of course, sundry legislative redefinitions of crime occur constantly. The monetary line between grand and petty theft may be redrawn on one occasion, and an attempt to assassinate a candidate for presidential office made a federal crime on another. However, these changes do not serve so much to change definitions of what is criminal as to alter jurisdiction over established crimes.

Much legislation in this country in the last century has regulated business activity. Much of the definition of violations has in this law been left to administrative rule-making bodies. Some crimes covered by the legislation, like anti-trust activity, have received a lot of attention but are absent in social-origins-of-law literature. This absence does seem to reflect one bias: to study why new definitions of crime are legislated only when the behavior defined—from theft to vagrancy to drinking to drug-taking to juvenile status offenses—can be seen, at least as likely as not, as working class behavior. Hence, social origins of legislation of criminal penalties for such behavior as entering into combinations in restraint of trade has not been a topic of social scientific concern. For the legislative process to have been studied, the behavior defined in the legislation studied, like drinking and drug use, need not be *exclusively* working class behavior, as long as it is not *exclusive of* working class behavior.

Having ruled out untenable rival explanations, it looks as though social scientists in our sample have chosen to study social origins of legislation that fairly represent leading kinds of substantive crime legislation—redefining behavior found at least in part among working classes—of its period. If substantive crime legislation in 14th-18th century England characteristically dealt with new kinds of property loss that employers of a changing economic order were suffering at the hands of their labor pool, then it is fair to conclude that the crime legislation originated in the overwhelming needs of a declining bourgeoisie on the one hand and an emerging bourgeoisie on the other to consolidate the political power they had over their workers. If crime legislation of the last hundred years in the United States has characteristically dealt with signs that social exchange is becoming meaningless for working class members as well as others, then it is fair to conclude that what Durkheim (1951:241-276) termed *anomie*—the feeling of being without rules to live by that he found arising among people when their economic order had begun to produce surplus goods and services—has inspired the legislation. Even an exceptional study of contemporary American legislation—that by McCaghy and Denisoff (1973) of changing the federal copyright law to include musical recordings—deals with competition for control of a commodity that could only rise to prominence in a surplus economy. The new forms of behavior we Americans have recently attended to in our crime legislation are not so much challenges to the economic hegemony of a bourgeoisie as challenges to the idea of economic and social interdependence in any form. While it appears that a source of legislation in 14th-18th century England may have been the force of concern of one class for consolidating its control over the other in a period of changing economic relationships, the corresponding source of legislation in our age in the United States appears the force of concern that economic and social exchange are not merely changing form, but are losing purpose for our lives in a surplus economy.

The distinctive feature of substantive crime legislation is that it redefines the need for people to be confined or restrained and hence tells us what kinds of failures of confinement or restraint are emerging as problems in a social order. This contrasts with other objectives of other kinds of legislation such as creating business incentives in tax law. The attention to new emerging problems is reflected in crime legislation of new problems of confinement which supplements and partially displaces attention to older problems. Pre-existing legislation is still enforced. People in the United States are still arrested, prosecuted, convicted, and confined for the kind of theft that was just being defined in 15th-century England, but this is an old, not new, problem.

GENERATING HYPOTHESES

The proposition that American crime legislation is currently shaped by anomie is admittedly tentative. The test of
the proposition will be in whether the hypotheses it implies
are refuted.

The studies in our literature sample already indicate
ambivalence about the wisdom of legislating confinement
and punishment as responses to anomie. Prohibition has
been repealed. Roby (1969) finds that the New York legislature has a hard time settling on a satisfactory response
to prostitution. Galliher et al. (1974) find the Nebraska
legislature deciding to retreat on its prior position that
marijuana possession should be harshly punished. And
there is a pejorative flavor to the descriptions of legislation
in all of the studies of contemporary American legislation
in our sample. Today in the United States, the ambivalence
in legislating against anomie is also reflected in the many
recommendations that so-called crimes without victims be
decriminalized (Morris and Hawkins, 1970; Packer, 1968).

This does not mean that our propensity to use punishment and confinement as a response to anomie is waning.
When legislatures lower penalties, they facilitate arrest and
prosecution for offenses, as Galliher et al. (1974) found to
be the case in Nebraska. At the same time the legislatures
are reacting toward some laws with what could be inter-
preted as disfavor or ambivalence, and they are unambiva-
lently strengthening other provisions, as in recent amend-
ments allowing small communities to use their own standards to convict, with impunity, people for propagating
obscenity. Like prostitution, what is regarded as obscene
material is generally that which symbolizes the detachment
of physical from social relations.

Ambivalence toward anomie-inspired legislation reflects
the futility of trying to combat anomie with confinement
and punishment. Those whose behavior is symptomatic of
anomie are acting out the purposelessness of their lives,
the superfluousness of their labor to social survival. When

this behavior is made criminal, the process can give purpose to the lives of those found guilty, to be sure. Those found guilty are given the task of resisting state deprivations of their lives, liberty, and property, and of trying to live down the stigma of their guilt. Criminalizing the symptoms of anomie can turn a subject of the law from having an asocial existence to having an antisocial mission, in the fashion that Lemert (1962) describes as the process of becoming paranoid. The legislative reaction to anomie compounds, not confines, the problem of a failure of positive social purpose in people's lives, making it seem more hopeless than ever that anomie can be transcended.

Hypothesis 1: *For the time being, the anomie-character of substantive American crime legislation will predominate more, not less. Accordingly, it will become increasingly difficult to see that anyone in particular is victimized by what is newly defined as criminal behavior.*[3] What might turn out to represent this trend has been the enactment of special penalties for engaging in organized crime, with the thought that organized crime becomes especially pernicious when it operates in the form of legitimate business. We probably have yet to see the limit to legislative participation in the blurring of the distinction between legitimate and illegitimate behavior.

Since anomie comes from having a surplus of human labor available in a society, we are led to Hypothesis 2.

Hypothesis 2: *Legislative preoccupation with anomie will diminish only as we move toward what we perceive to be full employment of members of our society.* As matters now stand, the trend is in the opposite direction. Little more than a decade ago, the President's Council of Economic Advisors first took the position that we had to accept a certain level of unemployment—4% of our work force— in the United States. Today, the argument is over whether this level should be raised to 6% or 7%.

There is a concept in physics known as entropy. As a system continues to operate, it generates its own unsystematic behavior, which ultimately must grow to such proportions that the system completely breaks down into disorder.

Hypothesis 3: *Because of the accumulation of entropy with growing anomie, the system of mutual feedback between crime legislation and signs of anomie will eventually break down and be superseded.*

As the system of legislating against anomie breaks down, the need for each person to work for his/her and others' survival should become obvious.

Hypothesis 4: *At this point, as in 15th-century England, legislative concern will turn to using confinement and punishment as tools to consolidate the control of some class or classes over others in a new and emerging system of economic relations.*

There is no theoretical basis for predicting when this transition will occur. All that can be said is that a turn in the direction of full employment is hypothesized to precede a shift in the kind of substantive crime legislation now characteristic of the United States, and that the new kind of crime legislation is hypothesized to be the property-loss kind characteristic of 15th-century England, but within the context of a new system of economic relations. Americans will find a way to sustain increases in levels of employment in the society, and when they do, the character of their substantive crime legislation will change, as a new economic system is synthesized out of the dialectic—between the meaninglessness of social life and a collective desire for social life to have meaning—currently at the leading edge of American political development.

It remains to be seen whether these predictions come true, or whether instead the knowledge of social origins of substantive criminal laws, gleaned from the studies we have sampled, will be refuted by the test of experience.

NOTES

1. By which we mean those laws concerning which behavior deserves state confinement or punishment, including, for instance, laws defining juvenile status

offenses and sexual psychopathy, as well as provisions of substantive criminal law. We considered including studies like Rusche and Kirchheimer's (1968), of procedural legislation, but found it too confusing to try to integrate studies of procedural law—defining *how* to confine people—with studies of substantive law—defining *what* to confine people for.

2. We could think of no systematic way to sample such an atomized literature. We see this paper as but the beginning of an ongoing inquiry into the topic, and we ask our readers to help us by bringing to our attention any important studies we have overlooked.

3. This difficulty—of showing that someone is injured by criminal behavior—is also characteristic of violations of business regulations, notably including antitrust violations (Pepinsky, 1976:29-32).

REFERENCES

BECKER, H.S. (1963). Outsiders: Studies in the sociology of deviance. New York: Free Press.

BEIER, A.L. (1974). "Vagrants in the social order in Elizabethan England." Past and Present 64 (August):3-29.

BONNIE, R.J. and WHITEBREAD, C.H. II (1974). The marijuana connection. Charlottesville: University of Virginia Press.

CHAMBLISS, W.J. (1964). "A sociological analysis of the law of vagrancy." Social Problems 12 (Summer): 67-77.

DICKSON, D.T. (1968). "Bureaucracy and morality: An organizational perspective on a moral crusade." Social Problems 16 (Fall):143-156.

DURKHEIM, E. (1951). Suicide: A study in sociology. [J.A. Spaulding and G. Simpson, trans.; G. Spaulding, ed.]. New York: Free Press.

DUSTER, T. (1970). The legislation of morality: Law, drugs, and moral judgment. New York: Free Press.

GALLIHER, J.F., McCARTNEY, J.L., and BAUM, B. (1974). "Nebraska's marihuana law: a case of unexpected legislative innovation." Law and Society Review 8 (Spring):441-455.

GALLIHER, J.F. and WALKER, A. (1977). "The puzzle of the origins of the Marihuana Tax Act of 1937." Social Problems 24 (February):367-376.

GRAHAM, J.M. (1972) "Amphetamine politics on Capitol Hill." Trans-action 9 (January):14-22, 53.

GUSFIELD, J.R. (1963). Symbolic crusade: Status politics and the American temperance movement. Urbana: University of Illinois Press.

HALL, J. (1952). Theft, law, and society. Indianapolis: Bobbs-Merrill.

HASKINS, G. (1960). Law and authority in early Massachusetts: A study in tradition and design. New York: Macmillan.

JEFFERY, C.R. (1957). "The development of crime in early English society." Journal of Criminal Law, Criminology, and Police Science 47 (March-April):647-666.

LEMERT, E.M. (1962). "Paranoia and the dynamics of exclusion." Sociometry 25 (March): 2-25.

——— (1972). Human deviance, social problems, and social control. Englewood Cliffs, N.J.: Prentice-Hall.

LINDESMITH, A.R. (1965). The addict and the law. Bloomington: Indiana University Press.

McCAGHY, C.H. and DENISOFF, A. (1973). "Pirates and politics: an analysis of interest group conflict." Pp. 297-309, in R.S. Denisoff and C.H. McCaghy (eds.), Deviance, conflict, and criminality. Chicago: Rand McNally.

MORRIS, N. and HAWKINS, G. (1970). The honest politician's guide to crime control. Chicago: University of Chicago Press.

MUSTO, D.F. (1973). The American disease: Origins of narcotics control. New Haven, Conn.: Yale University Press.

NELSON, W.E. (1967). "Emerging notions of modern criminal law in the revolutionary era: An historical perspective." New York University Law Review 42 (May):450-482.

PACKER, H.L. (1968). The limits of the criminal sanction. Stanford, Calif.: Stanford University Press.

PEPINSKY, H.E. (1976). Crime and conflict: A study of law and society. New York: Academic Press.

PLATT, A. (1969). The child-savers: The invention of delinquency. Chicago: University of Chicago Press.

QUINNEY, R. (1970). The social reality of crime. Boston: Little, Brown.

ROBY P.A. (1969). "Politics and criminal law: revision of the New York State law on prostitution." Social Problems 17 (Summer):83-109.

RUSCHE, G. and KIRCHHEIMER, O. (1968). Punishment and social structure. New York: Russell and Russell.

SELLIN, T. and WOLFGANG, E. (1964). The measurement of delinquency. New York: John Wiley.

SINCLAIR, A. (1962). Prohibition: The era of excess. Boston: Little, Brown.

SUTHERLAND, E.M. (1950). "The diffusion of sexual psychopath laws." American Journal of Sociology 56 (September):142-148.

TIMBERLAKE, J.H. (1963). Prohibition and the progressive movement: 1900-1920. Cambridge, Mass.: Harvard University Press.

Ruth-Ellen M. Grimes
Austin T. Turk
University of Toronto

3

LABELING IN CONTEXT
Conflict, Power, and
Self-Definition

Despite repeated challenges (Akers, 1968, 1973:16-26; Bordua, 1967; Gibbs, 1966, 1972; Gove, 1975; McCaghy, 1976:80-88; Tittle, 1975a, 1975b), proponents of the labeling perspective on deviance have responded less constructively than defensively (e.g., Goode, 1975; Kitsuse, 1975; Schur, 1971, 1975) to criticisms of their inattention to pertinent issues and problems, scanty production of intelligible and systematic propositions, and failure to provide criteria by which theoretical statements might be falsified. The burden of the defense has been that those using the labeling perspective simply have radically different aims and methods that render such criticisms inappropriate. However, with the critics we agree that it is not enough merely to offer labeling as a sensitizing concept that suggests what it *may* be like and feel like to be disapproved or punished. Sooner or later, sensitizing must pay off in more adequate (systematic, testable) formulations of *what* is to be explained, and *how*.

Whatever else it may be, the labeling perspective has generally been understood by both proponents and critics to be a statement that negative actions or reactions by other people somehow affect or *may* affect (the distinction is important in the debate) the beliefs and feelings individuals develop about themselves. The initial idea, derived from

39

symbolic interactionism, is that negative feedback is associated with socially unacceptable and/or personally un-
satisfying self-concepts. It has become clear that any such
statement must identify alternative outcomes of labeling
and specify the conditions under which each is likely to
occur. The question is, when and how does labeling affect
an individual's definition and evaluation of self?

An adequate answer, we believe, requires the explicit
incorporation of the idea of labeling into the larger perspective of structural conflict theory.[1] From Lemert (1951,
1974) and Becker (1963) to Lofland (1969), Matza (1964,
1969), and Schur (1971), analysts of labeling have, of
course, viewed it as a "conflict move" (in the parlance
of game theory) in which some more powerful party im-
poses its moral judgment upon a less powerful one. Nonetheless, it is unhelpful and misleading simply to postulate
that some less powerful people are stigmatized because
they arouse moral indignation (Becker, 1963:147-163;
Douglas, 1970), are "discreditable" (Goffman, 1963:3-4),
or are "strongly feared" (Lofland, 1969:14). Such relatively
uncomplicated formulations miss or obscure variations in
the structural sources and consequences of labeling and,
therefore, of variations in the impact of labeling upon those
who are labeled. As Davis (1972) has noted, the "social
conflict orientation . . . was incorporated as a fundamental
premise in labeling theory but did not greatly influence
research."

We take it as a sociological truism for critics as well as
proponents of the labeling perspective that deviance is a
socially created phenomenon—i.e., the socially defined
(explicitly in words or implicitly in nonrandom sanctioning)
violation of man-made and at least sometimes disputed
rules.[2] The "conflict process" or "conflict game" of creating
and attempting to control deviance evidently occurs in every
social relationship, from the most ephemeral dyadic encounters to the most complex relations among and within
the classes and other social structures of modern societies.
Specific variations in the impact of labeling upon self-
definition—as well as in other aspects of the process (here-
after "the deviance process")—are expected to be associ-

ated with variable features of the social context, most notably the scale and formality of its organization.[3]

THE DEVIANCE PROCESS IN INTRA-GROUP AND CROSS-GROUP CONTEXTS

For analytical convenience, contextual variation may be viewed as ranging from (1) a relatively small-scale informal setting in which people know and deal with one another personally as members of the same group to (2) a relatively large-scale formal structure in which people generally do not know one another and interact as agents or representatives of different groups. The deviance process in the first kind of social context is characteristically a matter of *intra-group* stigmatization and sanctioning. In the second kind of context the process is typically that of *inter*-group or, for clarity's sake, *cross-group* labeling.[4]

In both contexts the deviance process involves a *prior normative context* and five analytically distinct but empirically blended phases or dimensions: *identification, justification, negotiation, enclosure,* and *disposition.* With respect to each we suggest that there are modal differences between intra-group and cross-group labeling. After indicating what we see as the most salient differences, we consider the varying implications for self-definition by those subjected to labeling.

Prior Normative Context

Even though it is true that each human action and interaction is a uniquely constructed reality, it is also true that the tools and materials used in the construction are not all created on the spot (cf. Douglas, 1970: 12-19). The "reality models," the understandings of what is real, generated out of prior experiences, become tools and materials for selectively "having" subsequent ones. To the degree that the categories of meaningfulness defined by the models are charged with positive or negative significance, they constitute the normative context within which actions and encounters will be not only sensed or recognized but also evaluated. Though in practice more adapted than merely applied, such normative contexts thus precede any particular behavioral or interactional event.

The characteristic difference between intra-group and cross-group normative contexts appears to be that the former are less likely than the latter to be articulated in any systematic fashion. Normative understandings are in intra-group situations expected to be generally tacit, and invoked ad hoc by restricted language codes. In cross-group settings normative understandings seem far more likely to be (at least ostensibly) drawn from a list or system of propositions and expressed in elaborated language codes.[5] Reference in the intra-group case is likely to be to informal group norms; in the cross-group case it will more likely be to formal laws.

In both contexts the extent to which an eventual labelee shares the applicable normative understandings with the labelers is a basic contingency for self-definition. Tacit awareness of an informal group's normative context may mirror tacit acceptance by an individual of his/her position, and may extend to the person's own perception *and reflexive use* of the operative controls. In addition, that the individual is a more or less conscious member of a polity allows for a contextual placement *of the self by the self* in a politically organized society. The political power derivative from such a society does not arise from the power of a group but rather from the power that each individual imparts through action. The individual simultaneously grapples with normative context *within the self* as well as in interaction with labeling others.

Identification

Criteria for identifying deviance are contained or implied in normative contexts. Particular observed or imputed behavioral, relational, anatomical, mental, or spiritual attributes are taken to be *stigmata,* indicators of eligibility for placement in negatively evaluated categories. Initial or preliminary placement is accomplished by *typification* (implicit if not necessarily verbalized), i.e., the use of a very limited amount of information of unknown quality to confirm the presence of stigmata, and thereupon to classify persons or events. Instead of a stigma being a relationship between a stereotype and an attribute (Goffman, 1963:4), it seems rather that the relationship between an attribute and a stigma is a stereotype. In fact, it is most accurate to say that attributes, stigmata, and the linkages between them are *all* stereotypes. Actions and reactions are recognized and evaluated in generalizing terms set by on-going "behavioral constituencies" whose prior collective experiences tend to override or distort the particular features of immediate events.

Intra-group and cross-group identification differ in that typification appears likely to be clumsier in the latter, i.e., having a greater chance of challenge on grounds of irrelevancy and/or factual or procedural error. In intra-group labeling the criteria of deviance and the sufficiency of the evidence for initial placement are more likely to be accepted by everyone concerned, including the identified deviant.

Justification

After the flurry of initial identification, a more considered effort to justify the decision proceeds along two lines: empirical and theoretical. Empirically, the available evidence is generated by relatively objective (prototypically "legal") investigation and testing, even though the assessment is pervaded by the tendency through retrospective interpretation (Schur, 1971:52-56) for human beings to define away their mistakes or any discrepancies in perception and judgment. The effort to marshal theoretical justifications typically involves appealing to both common sense and scientific, medical, or legal doctrines.

Justification in intra-group contexts is marked by a heavy reliance upon the personal knowledge that members of a group (believe they) have about one another—as well as the self-confidence to match the "countervailing self" (Lemert, 1972:18), i.e., to neutralize any doubts they may have about what they are doing. Accordingly, empirical investigation tends to be informal and unconstrained by any exclusionary rules; theoretical rationales are most likely to be found in common sense. Though the validity of an identification may well be more assured by an untrammeled search for the truth, attribution of a serious violation to a person of law repute is almost certain to be justified. In cross-group justification technical considerations will probably be much more important than general personalized knowledge and common sense in the production of evidence and the formulation of rationales for identification. Despite the subtlety and complexity of technical procedures, the lack of interpersonal knowledge makes it impossible to develop the intricate mixtures of characterological, behavioral and situational analyses that frequently characterize intra-group justification. Administrative costs and political consider- ations usually preclude efforts to attain a really intimate knowledge of persons and circumstances; therefore, more determinate facts and more universally understandable arguments are likely to be used in defending or contesting the identification of a deviant person or event.

Negotiation

The pressure upon the accused to participate actively in the deviance process is especially strong in regard to confirming and refining the initial identification. Accusing others typically use persuasive instead of overtly coercive techniques in trying to induce identified deviants to partici- pate in their own stigmatization. "Plea bargaining" in the broadest sense means drawing the accused into cooperat- ing by agreeing to be questioned or examined, with the implication that anomalies may and will be used to deter- mine the precise nature of his/her deviance. Such cooper- ation helps to allay any doubts the accusers may have, and thus sustain the assumptions of self-righteousness, crafts- manship, or unavoidable necessity by which people ration- alize their moral policing of others. "Successful" negotia- tion of a deviant identification is marked by the deviant's loss of confidence in personal autonomy and capacity. Radical shifts in the individual's sense of self may occur (at least after repeated processing); but the more usual accomplishment is the introduction of self-doubt to the point of convincing the person that there is no alternative to accepting stigmatization. The issue becomes not *whether* but *how* and with what consequences s/he is to be classified as a deviant.

Intra-group negotiation is less constrained than cross-group negotiation by explicit bargaining rules, which makes it easier both to carry out a successful negotiation and for the parties involved to explore the full range of circumstances and outcomes, including exoneration. Control agents typically rely upon and appeal to group *participation* as a *value* for the accused, with lesser reliance upon expediency arguments and greater emphasis upon their desire to help at least a penitent if not innocent fellow group member. Because control agents in cross-group contexts usually have to negotiate from positions of relative weakness in terms of personal familiarity with the accused, bargaining tends to be more impersonal, with hypocritical concern for the individual expressed mainly to gain negotiating leverage. Appeals to expediency are standard, with stress upon the inescapable *fact* of "group" *membership.* Success in intra-group negotiation typically presupposes the authenticity of concern and cooperation, but successful cross-group negotiation presupposes only the inability of the deviant to resist the threats and/or tricks of the accusers.

Lofland's (1969:14) reference to small groups as threats to larger ones acquires greater rationality, as well as irony, when considered in reference to the relatively weak position of cross-group control agents in negotiating deviant identity. The rationality lies in the threat which psychologically integrated groups can pose to larger organizations lacking cohesion. The irony lies in the fact that the individual is subject to a government comprised of individuals who act within a political normative context to which they themselves are subject and to which they cannot always conform, if only because their own actions cannot always coincide entirely with the expectations of others—including their fellow control agents. *Any* particular individual is ultimately a "minority group" vis-à-vis the "majority group" that is the polity.

Enclosure

Enclosure is the phase in deviance processing in which doubts have been resolved and accusing others act so as to mark off the line between respectability and deviance (Douglas, 1970) in the specific case. The decision is announced by action and probably in some fashion by words that a deviation has been identified, the identification justified, and the deviant event or individual appropriately classified. If responsibility for the deviant case has been affixed to someone, the now confirmed deviant is subjected to the closing off of normal opportunities for interaction (Cohen, 1965). The effect is to enclose the deviant in a social representation or analogue of the meaning category into which s/he has been placed. Physical, social, or symbolic barriers are erected between the labelee and the labelers, including the deviant's own countervailing self.

In intra-group settings enclosure involves a characteristically more subtle interaction in which there is proportionately greater use of symbolic and social barriers. Even the use of physical restraints is often more subtle than in cross-group enclosure—i.e., more likely to be achieved by such tactics as withdrawal from the deviant (e.g., leaving the deviant alone, shutting a door, refusal to make or keep appointments with her/him); confiscation of facilities needed for interaction (e.g., keys, tools, uniforms); or construction of largely symbolic physical obstacles to interaction (e.g., fences, hedges, repositioned furniture). At least up to the final decision about disposition of the case, the components of enclosure are likely to be more intricately blended in intra-group than in cross-group contexts. Violence, in particular, is likely to be used later and less frequently in the deviance process. The individual's participation in his/her own enclosure (as in self-imposed hermitage) seems more probable in intra-group settings, and more likely to constitute a kind of adaptation that allows her/him to live at variance with the normative context, yet without a challenge to it being recognized by self or others.

Disposition

The final phase is the determination of whether the deviant is to be permanently enclosed. The decision may be formally or informally verbalized, or may only be implied by the way in which enclosure is accomplished. Whether or not overt, the emphasis in disposition may be more rehabilitative or more punitive; and the outcomes may be rehabilitation, termination, or institutionalization.

If the deviant has been cooperative in providing confessional recognition of her/his deviance, rehabilitation is more likely to be emphasized. If not, punishment can be expected to receive more emphasis. Regardless of the relative emphasis, the sanctioning implicit in the deviance process means that some punishment is certain, while rehabilitation obviously is not. Indeed, it is questionable whether an individual who has been fully processed can be fully restored socially, in the sense that interaction is neither presently nor potentially affected by the person's record of deviance.

Termination may be achieved by exile or execution, and is the ultimate form of enclosure. In principle, termination is irreversible; once ejected, the individual is no longer even a deviant—someone who must be dealt with—but rather a nonentity who ceases to be an impelling reality. Other cases and concerns become the points upon which the available human energies are focused in carrying on the eternal process of stigmatization and sanctioning.

Between the extremes of rehabilitation and termination, and having elements of both, is institutionalization. The deviant is neither terminated nor restored to social normalcy, but is relegated to a permanently inferior status as a "career" deviant. As such, the person is (probably tacitly) expected and pressed to provide evidence of his/her deviant *character,* specifically by acquiring the behavioral, relational, and other attributes deemed appropriate for the kind of person s/he is now presumed to be. Career deviants in some form are found in all social contexts, whether because they are "functional" as horrible examples and as providers of illicit goods and services (i.e., "relevant . . . in the community's overall division of labor"—Erikson, 1966:19), or merely because career deviance is finally synonymous with social inferiority. To be lower class is to be deviant in the eyes of those belonging to the higher classes.

Intra-group is more likely than cross-group disposition to reflect a greater concern with the possibility of rehabilitation. At the same time, rejection of the recalcitrant, the unrepentant sinner, is more likely to be charged with genuine moral indignation than in cross-group contexts, where termination will be as much a political as a moral matter. Moreover, cross-group contexts seem to provide more possibilities for institutionalization, because greater social differentiation implies the existence of more opportunities and demands for the exchange of illicit as well as licit goods and services.

Apparently the most fundamental difference between intra-group and cross-group deviance processing is that the former involves far greater concern for the fate of the individual. There is a working assumption in intra-group contexts that the individual case is worth the effort to process it, and there is a proportionately greater expenditure of time and other resources per case. The relative superficiality of the deviance process in cross-group contexts is evident: the individual case is much less important than the machinery for processing cases (e.g., Balbus, 1973). While in intra-group settings the primary objective is *person* control, in cross-group contexts it is *population* control.

Our review of contextual differences in the deviance process suggests several ways in which the ideas of labeling and conflict complement each other within the framework of structural conflict theory. Each provides a means of noting and analyzing particular aspects of the process:

(1) Labeling: the problematic relationship between normative context and human behavior and relations. Conflict: the

implications of that *problematique* in terms of variability in moral understandings among the members of a group and in normative contexts among groups.

(2) Labeling: the transformation of abstract normative categories into living examples in the course of the deviance process. Conflict: the contingencies that make such transformations problematic instead of inevitable.

(3) Labeling: the social psychological dynamics of interaction in the process, within as well as among the interacting selves. Conflict: the structural sources and ramifications of, and constraints upon, that interaction.

(4) Labeling: the significance of perceptual and normative consensus and collaboration between accused and accusers in affecting the course of the deviance process. Conflict: the significance of dissensus and the relative power of accusers and accused in affecting the course of the process.

SELF-DEFINITION AND THE
CONTEXT OF LABELING

Because labeling analysts have typically treated deviant behavior merely as symptomatic of an identity acquired in a helpless reaction to arbitrary labeling, alternative possibilities have been neglected (cf. Thorsell and Klemke, 1972): (1) that behavior and self-definition may vary independently; (2) that labeling may have no significant effect upon an individual's conception of self; (3) that individuals may in the absence of labeling choose deviant acts and even deviant careers as meaningful forms of self-expression; (4) that labeling may deter instead of promote deviant behavior; and (5) that labeling may be considered rather than arbitrary, and considered more in reference to population control (general deterrence) than to person control (specific deterrence). In contrast, concern with all of these possibilities as issues is inherent in the conflict perspective, because deviant behavior is treated not as symptomatology but as the means by which individuals singly and collectively try to enhance their lives despite the normative expectations of others, who are presumed to be engaged in doing the same thing. Whether normative expectations are reasonable or essential is considered to depend more upon whose values and interests are given priority than upon any conceptions of moral or functional necessity.

From the conflict perspective, labeling is necessarily a *relational* as well as a *processual* concept. It makes sense only in terms of an interaction occurring in a particular kind of social context. Unless the context of labeling is specified, the concept itself is meaningless for the conflict analysts, since "almost every conceivable dimension of human behavior is considered deviant from the normative perspective of some existing persons and groups" (Simmons, 1965).

As a *politically* constructed reality, deviance cannot be readily dichotomized into primary and secondary types, nor can the attributes of a deviant be designated in other than contextual terms.[6] For instance, Lofland's (1969:39-41) distinction between "defensive" and "adventurous" deviance dissolves into ambiguity in the absence of contextual specification. Certainly there is no basis for characterizing a "deviant" kind of self in the abstract. In Kaplan's words (1975:56), "a behavior pattern is not deviant by virtue of the fact that it serves, or is intended to serve attack, avoidance, or substitutive functions towards the goal of self-enhancement. Nor is the behavior necessarily deviant because it takes these forms."

Instead of a self stripped of autonomy in the irresistible push from primary into secondary deviance, the conflict analyst posits a self *acting* on its own behalf, not simply *reacting* (even in anticipation) to the expectations or demands of other people. In acting, and thereby creating behaviors independently, the self confronts the countervailing self, the notion of which has all too often been riddled with incorrect and misplaced negative connotations. Perhaps it is within this notion of a largely negativistic countervailing self that labeling theorists have gone awry. This seemingly passive reactor, admitting to behavior deviant in the society, serves as the focal point for the notion that the group affects the individual and has the *power* to change his/her actions. The key is lost if one assumes that the position of the countervailing self was not originally one of choice, arrived at in a personally conflictive manner given the political structure as the overwhelming source of conflict. Ericson (1975:83-87) has touched upon the question of the labeled individual's own part in the labeling process, emphasizing "the dialectic between the self-concept and behavior" (p. 87). Ericson further notes that "the idea of 'self-labelling' has become an important part of analysis, showing the way in which the deviant actively constructs and presents a view of his self, and so fundamentally affects the way he is labelled socially" (p. 145).

In short, the process of self-definition is seen as occurring *in* various contexts without necessarily being determined *by* the context in which it occurs. This does not mean that self-definition is totally independent of social context; rather, the point is that connection is viewed as entirely problematic.

Analysis of the self-definition process begins with locating the individual in reference to the linkage between *personal* power (the resources of the individual as such— e.g., intellect, beauty, charm, strength) and *political* power (the resources available to the individual by virtue of group and organizational attachments). Given an assessment of the individual's power, the task is to relate the "subjective problems" of the individual actor's self-definition, consciousness, and choice, to the "objective problems" of his or her interaction with others in contexts of interpersonal and inter-group conflict.

Labeling analysts such as Lofland (1969) and Schur (1971) have, as noted previously, pointed out that political power is involved in the deviance process; but they have relegated the political component to either the rule-making stage or the organizational processing stage. Yet it is at the juncture of personal and political power that the process of self-definition occurs, not in any neat sequence but in a complex simultaneity of action and reaction, behaving and labeling. Here the crucial facts are generated by the person engaging in self-defining behavior with some probability of collision with other persons similarly engaged. No outcome is assured, no conclusion foregone. Even against seemingly overwhelming intra-group and/or cross-group forces, the autonomy of the individual may not only persist (cf. Matza, 1969:144-180), but may even be extended to the point of "usurping" the power of the contending group or organization.

The self, then, as an initiator and effector of change, as an autonomous entity, holds a power position at least potentially threatening to any group from the smallest to the largest in scale, and from the least to the most formally organized and hierarchical. It is in this sense that Lofland's conception becomes apt: that deviants are persons labeled because they are feared by persons with more power (Lofland, 1969:14). It is not that the fear is necessarily there, as Lofland asserts, but that it probably should be. Whenever a group or organization comes into conflict with an individual's self-enhancing enterprise, the consequence may be not the "control" of that enterprise but incorporation of the group or organization into it. Instead of being subjugated, the individual may recruit the would-be controllers, or labelers, to his or her cause.

Himelfarb (1975) has argued that the labeling perspective's emphasis on "master labelers" obscures the essential role of the primary actor. He states (1975:22) that "it must be recognized that actors who are being offered new definitions of self already possess self-definitions. In studying self-change, then, we must examine how actors' present self-definitions influence their acceptance of new definitions." This statement, though clearly an advance over the situational determinism of most labeling accounts, presupposes that new "master statuses" are being presented "externally" and may be imposed by master labelers who are obviously powerful influences in the actor's life. Himelfarb does not go on to entertain the possibility that the actor may "internally" produce a new or revised self-definition that leads to changes in "external" labeling by others.

Master labelers are only indirectly the agents of stability or change in self-definitions. Whatever they propose must interact with, and may be outweighed by, the person's internal master status and pattern of "role engulfment."[7] Labeling by others is significant only to the extent that it "fits," or complements individuals' labeling of themselves. It is because the chances of complementarity are greater in intra-group social contexts than in cross-group ones that labeling by one's regular associates can generally be expected to have more effect upon self-definition than will labeling by comparative strangers.

Following Mead, Shibutani (1962:141) has suggested that "one's choice of definitions depends upon one's sentiments toward significant others." One can interpret this as the labeling analysts seem generally to have done: a self-definition is invoked by others in reaction to the person's actions, and is accepted because they are somehow "significant." Or, as the conflict perspective suggests, the interpretation may be that the person chooses before acting, and on the basis of perceptions, reconstructions, and rehearsals of both (a) the self interacting with others, and (b) peers ("like me") interacting with others. The question is: what is significant about those others?

Though agreeing that others must be significant (almost by definition) to affect self-definition, we do not accept that the first step in research is to select the significant others (cf. Himelfarb, 1975) according to what they appear to be doing, or capable of doing, with or to the subject of interest. It is inconsistent to launch an inquiry into the *selection* of others if one has already defined a set of master labelers (e.g., family, peers, courts, police) as self-evident. Instead, one is led to ascertain the individual's perceptions of the quality of her or his relations to intra-group associates and to cross-group control agents. Neither the psychological or emotional significance nor the power significance of either intra-group or cross-group others can be taken for granted —especially since the individual's own selection of others is not arbitrarily determined by their objective significance, but depends upon their subjective, functional significance at particular moments or intervals. The individual has to be psychologically as well as situationally located in relation to the social contexts, intra-group and cross-group, in which s/he is found.

To locate the individual in context requires knowledge of how any operative "fronts" s/he may employ are linked to her or his understandings or versions of self and of the outside world. Whether either intra-group or cross-group interactions culminate in an altered self-definition is contingent upon the success of the "conflict moves" made by the individual in contention with others whose self-enhancing enterprises impinge upon his or her own. Successful moves are those in which the person uses or rejects the imputations of others, whichever is more compatible with the aim of self-enhancement. This image of the person as an actor seeking self-enhancement is congenial with Kaplan's (1975:10) conception of "the self-esteem motive," which is defined as "the need of the person to maximize the experience of positive self-attitudes and to minimize the experience of negative self-attitudes or self-feelings." (However, the nature and source of the posited "need" are so ambiguous that we prefer not to commit ourselves to the notion that people *need* to do something which they *do* in any case.)

Goode (1975) and Sagarin (1976) have recently emphasized the point that the imputation of identities tends to preclude meaningful interaction, as well as theoretical understanding of what is going on. Rather than jumping from behavioral observations to impute supposedly corresponding identities, the analyst is challenged to deal with the empirical problem of determining how a person's behavior is related to the on-going enterprise of self-definition.

CONCLUSION

The conflict perspective frees labeling analysis from the deterministic reactive trap into which it has too often fallen. The full range of interaction outcomes is recognized, especially in reasserting the significance of the individual's own personal and political power in furthering her/his enterprise of self-definition. The complementarity of others' definitions with the individual's own is viewed as wholly problematic, and determined as much by the person's subjective or internal assessments as by the objective or external assessments of others. Others are not automatically significant in either psychological or power terms; their significance is a function of how their self-defining activities complement or conflict with the person's own. The effect of labeling upon self-definition depends upon the relative power of each involved individual, as each impinges upon the others in the course of the highly personal enterprise of self-definition. To be empirically useful, the labeling idea has to be extended to *all* the labeling going on in an individual's life, including of self and *of* others as well as the labeling *by* others.

As the labeling idea is extended beyond the preoccupation with deviance to the general processes of interaction and interdependency between persons and groups, it becomes useful in a theoretical explanation of the conflict found in any political-legal context. Labeling theory ties into conflict theory to the extent that the struggle for power constitutes the contingencies for action and reaction. The individual qualifies her/his sense of autonomy when s/he encounters the contingencies posed by variations in power as the basic fact of social life. The struggle sets the arena for behavioral reaction; personal action is mitigated by the self's recognition of other selves as limiting factors. In the merger of arena and action the quality of the person's behavior and self is shaped and sustained.

Whatever may be the strengths and limitations of a perspective integrating the labeling and conflict ideas, it is clear that we

> are not likely to come up with a complete explanation of deviant behavior in general until we tie it into a general theory of social behavior. By the same token, the study of societal control of deviance must be tied to the larger study and theory of conflict, power and norm formation and enforcement. [Akers, 1968:464]

NOTES

1. For the most general recent statement, see Collins (1975). Among students of deviance and social control, the conflict perspective has been developed mainly by criminologists such as Vold (1958), Turk (1969), Taylor et al. (1973), Quinney (1975), and Chambliss (1976), though Lofland (1969) does begin his general deviance text by characterizing deviance as a "conflict game."

2. To be sure, some critics (Hirschi, 1973, 1975; Wellford, 1975; and Gove, 1970, 1975) have apparently been baited into almost denying that deviance is a problematic social construct.

3. Thorsell and Klemke (1972) emphasize the importance of distinguishing "between official, institutionalized reactions to deviant acts and the informal reactions of one's significant others."

4. Our purpose here is to systematize numerous empirical generalizations found in or suggested by the standard literatures on criminality, deviance, social control, and law. Thus, we neither claim great originality for any specific proposition nor find it necessary to attempt to substantiate each statement by detailed substantive references. Our choice of the term "the deviance process" is intended to emphasize that we see deviance not as a simple product of one-way deterministic labeling, but rather as a complex, problematic outcome of a two-way conflictual interaction between parties whose relative power decides who is to be labeler and who labelee.

5. On the distinction between restricted and elaborated language codes, see Bernstein (1966).

6. In the most general sense, *political* may be taken to mean the manipulative or dominating dimension of social interaction. Regarding the distinction between primary and secondary types, Lemert (1967:17) writes:

> Primary deviation is assumed to arise in a wide variety of social, cultural, and psychological contexts, and at best has only marginal implication for the psychic structure of the individual; it does not lead to symbolic recognition at the level of self-regarding attitudes and social roles. Secondary deviation is deviant behavior or social roles based upon it, which becomes a means of defense, attack or adaptation to the overt and covert problems created by the societal reaction to primary deviation.

Lemert's distinction appears to be untenable. If primary deviation involves "only marginal implication" for "self-regarding attitudes," then how do we explain secondary deviation arising in response to the societal reaction to primary deviation? Adequate explanation seems to require that the labelee adopt a more than marginally active and reactive attitude.

7. Hughes (1945) defined "master status" as "that one aspect of an individual which may be judged both by others and by himself to be the essential aspect of his identity in most situations."

The term "role engulfment" is used by Schur to refer to the point at which a person "caught up in" a deviant role finds "that it has become highly salient in his overall personal identity (or concept of self), that his behavior is increasingly organized around' the role, and that cultural expectations attached to the role have come to have precedence, or increased salience relative to other expectations, in the organization of his activities and general way of life" (1971:69).

REFERENCES

AKERS, R.L. (1968). "Problems in the sociology of deviance: Social definitions and behavior." Social Forces 46(June):455-465.

—— (1973). Deviant behavior: A social learning approach. Belmont, Calif.: Wadsworth.

BALBUS, I.D. (1973). The dialectics of legal repression. New York: Russell Sage.

BECKER, H.S. (1963). Outsiders: Studies in the sociology of deviance. New York: Free Press.

BERNSTEIN, B. (1966). "Elaborated and restricted codes: An outline." Sociological Inquiry 36(Spring):254-261.

BORDUA, D. (1967). "Recent trends: Deviant behavior and social control." Annals of the American Academy of Political and Social Science 369(January):149-163.

CHAMBLISS, W.J. (1976). "Functional and conflict theories of crime: The heritage of Emile Durkheim and Karl Marx." Pp. 1-28 in W.J. Chambliss and M. Mankoff (eds.), Whose law, what order? New York: John Wiley.

COHEN, A.K. (1965). "The sociology of the deviant act: Anomie theory and beyond." American Sociological Review 30(February):9-14.

COLLINS, R. (1975). Conflict sociology: Toward an explanatory science. New York: Academic Press.

DAVIS, N.J. (1972). "Labeling theory in deviance research: A critique and reconsideration." Sociological Quarterly 13(Autumn):447-474.

DOUGLAS, J.D. (1970). "Deviance and respectability: The social construction of moral meanings." Pp. 3-30 in J.D. Douglas (ed.), Deviance and respectability. New York: Basic Books.

ERICSON, R.V. (1975). Criminal reactions: The labelling perspective. Lexington, Mass.: D. C. Heath.

ERIKSON, K.T. (1966). Wayward puritans. New York: John Wiley.

GIBBS, J.P. (1966). "Conceptions of deviant behavior: The old and the new." Pacific Sociological Review 9(Spring):9-14.

—— (1972). "Issues in defining deviant behavior." Pp. 39-68 in R.A. Scott and J. Douglas (eds.), Theoretical perspectives on deviance. New York: Basic Books.

GOFFMAN, E. (1963). Stigma. Englewood Cliffs, N.J.: Prentice-Hall.

GOODE, E. (1975). "On behalf of labeling theory." Social Problems 22(June): 570-583.

GOVE, W.R. (1970). "Societal reaction as an explanation of mental illness: An evaluation." American Sociological Review 35(October):873-884.

—— (1975). "The labelling perspective: An overview." Pp. 3-20 in W.R. Gove (ed.), The labelling of deviance. Beverly Hills, Calif.: Sage.

HIMELFARB, A. (1975). Fat man, thin world. Ph.D. dissertation, University of Toronto. (unpublished)

HIRSCHI, T. (1973). "Procedural rules and the study of deviant behavior." Social Problems 21(Fall):159-173.

—— (1975). "Labeling theory and juvenile delinquency: An assessment of the evidence." Pp. 181-203 in W.R. Gove (ed.), The labelling of deviance. Beverly Hills, Calif.: Sage.

HUGHES, E.C. (1945). "Dilemmas and contradictions of status." American Journal of Sociology 50(March):353-359.

KAPLAN, H.B. (1975). Self-attitudes and deviant behavior. Pacific Palisades, Calif.: Goodyear.

KITSUSE, J. (1975). "The 'new conception of deviance' and its critics." Pp. 273-284 in W.R. Gove (ed.), The labelling of deviance. Beverly Hills, Calif.: Sage.
LEMERT, E.M. (1951). Social pathology. New York: McGraw-Hill.
——— (1967). "The concept of secondary deviation." Pp. 40-64 in Human deviance, social problems, and social control. Englewood Cliffs, N.J.: Prentice-Hall.
——— (1972). "Social problems and the sociology of deviance." Pp. 3-25 in human deviance, social problems, and social control. Englewood Cliffs, N.J.: Prentice-Hall (second edition).
——— (1974). "Beyond Mead: The societal reaction to deviance." Social Problems 21(April):457-468.
LOFLAND, J. (1969). Deviance and identity. Englewood Cliffs, N.J.: Prentice-Hall.
MATZA, D. (1964). Delinquency and drift. New York: John Wiley.
——— (1969). Becoming deviant. Englewood Cliffs, N.J.: Prentice-Hall.
McCAGHY, C.H. (1976). Deviant behavior. New York: Macmillan.
QUINNEY, R. (1975). Criminology. Boston: Little, Brown.
SAGARIN, E. (1976). "The high personal cost of wearing a label." Psychology Today (March):25-32.
SCHUR, E.M. (1971). Labeling deviant behavior. New York: Harper & Row.
——— (1975). "Comments." Pp. 285-294 in W.R. Gove (ed.), The labelling of deviance. Beverly Hills, Calif.: Sage.
SHIBUTANI, T. (1962). "Reference groups and social control." Pp. 128-145 in A.M. Rose (ed.), Human behavior and social processes. Boston: Houghton Mifflin.
SIMMONS, J.L. with Chambers, H. (1965). "Public stereotypes of deviants." Social Problems 13(Fall):223-232.
TAYLOR, I., WALTON, P., YOUNG, J. (1973). The new criminology. London: Routledge & Kegan Paul.
THORSELL, B.A. and KLEMKE, L.W. (1972). "The labelling process: Reinforcement and deterrent?" Law and Society Review 6(February):393-403.
TITTLE, C.R. (1975a). "Deterrents or labeling?" Social Forces 53(March):399-410.
——— (1975b) "Labeling and crime: An empirical evaluation." Pp. 159-179 in W.R. Gove (ed.), The labelling of deviance. Beverly Hills, Calif.: Sage.
TURK, A.T. (1969). Criminality and legal order. Chicago: Rand McNally.
VOLD, G. (1958). Theoretical criminology. New York: Oxford.
WELLFORD, C. (1975). "Labelling theory and criminology: An assessment." Social Problems 22(February):332-345.

Victoria Lynn Swigert
Holy Cross College

Ronald A. Farrell
State University of New York, Albany

4

REFERENT OTHERS AND DEVIANCE CAUSATION
A Neglected Dimension in Labeling Research

Since its popularization in the mid-1960s, the labeling perspective has attracted a great deal of criticism for its apparent inability to validate empirically its own core assumptions. Much of the research generated by the approach suggests that, contrary to the prediction, application of the deviant label is not a sufficient condition in the creation of deviant careers. At the same time, it may be argued that these findings illustrate not so much the poverty of the theoretical model as they do a neglect and inadequate operationalization of its more implicit assumptions. Through its failure to include reference identification and association in analyses of deviance causation, labeling research departs significantly from its theoretical antecedents and, therefore, from a satisfactory test of the labeling approach.

Labeling theory (Tannenbaum, 1938; Lemert, 1951; Becker, 1963; Scheff, 1966; Schur, 1971) as well as theories of reference identification and association (Sutherland, 1947; Glaser, 1956; Burgess and Akers, 1968; DeLamater, 1968) have their origins in symbolic interactionism. Such approaches, therefore, build upon the fundamental assumption that social reality is symbolically constructed. Through interaction in ongoing social activities, definitions are acquired which have implications for the identities and behaviors of participants. These perspectives differ, however, with regard to the emphasis accorded associational learning in explanations of nonconformity. The symbolic communication of deviant behavior patterns is most explicit in reference identification and association theories. Variations in the exposure of individuals to definitions favorable and unfavorable to norm violations, along with the cost-reward balance attending the acquired behaviors, account for variations in commitment to deviance and conformity. The importance of these factors remains implicit within labeling theory and is systematically neglected within labeling research. Rather, of primary concern are the processes by which certain individuals are designated as deviant and the consequences of such designations for future behavior.

A review of the labeling theory of nonconformity, and especially its research tradition, is both illustrative of the neglect of its theoretical antecedents and suggestive of means by which reference identification and association may be incorporated into empirical explorations of the approach.

THE INTERACTIONIST PERSPECTIVE

The underlying assumption of the interactionist approach is that awareness of self is made possible by the symbolic communication of the individual with significant others. Individual identity becomes meaningful only in reference to the responses of such persons. Thus, Cooley (1902) and Mead (1934) have argued that the individual does not experience the self directly but only by becoming an object to himself by assuming the attitudes of those in interaction with him. Drawing from Cooley's original conceptualization:

> A self-idea of this sort seems to have three principal elements: the imagination of our appearance to the other person; the imagination of his judgement of that appearance; and some sort of self-feeling, such as pride or mortification. [1902:183-184]

Perceiving disapproval in the reactions of others may be the source of negative self-evaluations. "If failure or disgrace arrives, if one suddenly finds that the faces of men show coldness or contempt instead of . . . kindness and deference, . . . he will perceive from the shock, the fear, the sense of being outcast and helpless" (Cooley, 1902: 208). Cooley pointed out that those possessing deviant aims or attributes are particularly subject to such negative self-feelings (pp. 259-260).

It is on this point that labelists have constructed their theory of deviance causation. Here too we find attention to the role of significant others in the process of deviance creation. Thus, Tannenbaum (1938:16-21), whose early work on crime and delinquency is often thought to be a forerunner of labeling theory, argued that the person's perception of the community's designation of him as deviant leads to the development of a criminal self-concept, and eventually to an identification and integration with a group which shares his activities. Tannenbaum further emphasized that in dealing with the offender, "We are dealing with a human being who is responding normally to the demands, stimuli, approval, expectancy, of the group with whom he is associated. . . . That group must exist or the criminal could not exist."

For Lemert (1951) as well, assuming a deviant role implies associational learning. "There must be a spreading corroboration of a socio-pathic self-conception and societal reinforcement at each step in the process" (Lemert, 1951: 77). Such corroboration depends on more than the negative reactions of agents of social control. Thus, deviance creation is not only the propulsion of the actor into the role of the outsider but involves his attraction to those willing to define the behavior in question in more positive terms.

Illustrative of this process is Becker's (1963) description of becoming a marijuana user. He explains that adopting such behavior involves more than the formal or informal assignment of an individual to a deviant status.

Before engaging in the activity on a more or less regular basis, the person has no notion of the pleasures to be derived from it, he learns these in the course of interaction with more experienced deviants. He learns to be aware of

new kinds of experiences and to think of them as pleasur-
able. . . . The individual *learns,* in short, to participate in a
subculture organized around the particular deviant activity.
[p. 31]

In association, behaviors defined negatively by society may
take on a more positive character, new rationales for continuing the behavior are acquired, and individuals learn
how to engage in the deviation with a "minimum of trouble"
and with enforcement evasion techniques established by
"earlier pioneers" (Becker, 1963:39).

Scheff (1966:84-87) likewise points out that it is through
social support that initially undifferentiated deviance is
transformed into more uniform and stable mental disorder.
He states that those comprising the treatment setting,
physicians and hospital personnel, as well as other patients,
reward the individual for conforming to their conceptions
of mental illness.

Pointing to the centrality of association within labeling
theory, Schur (1971) also observes that "involvement in the
subculture facilitates access to and immersion in deviant
roles that 'members' either feel a need for or find pleasur-
able or desirable" (p. 77). In like manner, theoretical developments in such diverse substantive areas as nudism
(Weinberg, 1966), stuttering (Lemert, 1962), homosexuality
(Farrell and Morrione, 1975), and blindness (Scott, 1969)
are unambiguous in their focus on the associational acqui-
sition of deviant behavior.

It appears, therefore, that labeling theorists are indeed
aware of the importance of referent others in the construction of deviant careers. Attention is given not only to the
perceived or real responses of legitimate society but to
identification and association with deviant groups as well.
In this conceptualization, persistent nonconformity is a
product both of the negative sanctions imposed by society
and of the interactional rewards provided by those similarly
labeled (DeLamater, 1968). Such theoretical efforts, however, differ considerably from attempts at empirical valida-
tion of the labeling approach.

LABELING RESEARCH

The labeling perspective on social deviance has yielded

essentially two distinct research emphases. The first, the societal reactions approach, is primarily concerned with organizational and interpersonal responses to nonconformity. Findings indicate quite clearly that a number of factors contribute to societal reactions to deviants. Cultural and subcultural definitions of deviance (Simmons, 1965; Reed and Reed, 1973; Shoemaker et al., 1973; Swigert and Farrell, 1976, 1977), the social characteristics of individuals (Gibbs, 1962; Goldman, 1963; Cameron, 1964; Skolnick, 1966; Farrell and Morrione, 1974), the circumstances under which they conduct their behavior (Stinchcombe, 1963; Chambliss and Liell, 1966), the nature of the behavior itself (Mechanic, 1962; Phillips, 1963; Larkin and Loman, 1977), and the sources of deviance imputations, such as family, friends, or organizational representatives (Mechanic, 1962; Phillips, 1963; Farrell and Morrione, 1974; Ericson, 1977) have all been shown to influence such reaction. Furthermore, the research suggests that once individuals are identified as members of disvalued categories, they may be stigmatized in all succeeding interaction with conforming others (Schwartz and Skolnick, 1962; Phillips, 1963; Loman and Larkin, 1976).

The second research emphasis focuses on the consequences of stigmatization for the behavior and identity of labeled deviants. It is this later tradition that is of concern to the present work. The underlying thesis of research in this area is that rejection of persons for evidence of nonconformity may lead to increased deviation. According to Lemert (1951), if nonconformity is severely sanctioned, it may be incorporated as part of the *me* of the individual. If, as a result, existing legitimate roles are disrupted, the individual may come to reorganize his life around the deviant identity. Lemert refers to this outcome as secondary deviation and suggests that it develops as a means of adjustment to the problems created by the societal reaction to the original or specific (primary) deviation.

Operationalization of Lemert's argument, however, has been limited. Most typically, a model is proposed that posits a direct, linear relationship between the application of formal sanctions and increased behavioral deviation. At best, the results of such studies are mixed. While evidence does exist to suggest the direct effect of official sanction on increased nonconformity (Gold and Williams, 1969; Meade, 1974; Farrington, 1977), an equivalent amount of research indicates quite the contrary (Williams and Weinberg, 1971; Fisher, 1972; Klein, 1974).[1]

The most outstanding feature of these efforts, in addition to the contradictory nature of their findings, is the systematic exclusion of the role of referent others from the analysis. Contrary to both symbolic interactionism and labeling theory itself, others have been largely defined as those who apply official sanction: the police, the courts, and the prisons.

Recognizing the centrality of referent others to the labeling perspective, Hepburn (1975) has commented that ''although social control agencies have been defined as the critical audience in sanctioning and labeling deviant behavior, an audience of significant others appears to be more crucial in the organization of deviant identity'' (Hepburn, 1975:393). Such an audience need not, after all, agree with the control agency concerning the applicability of the label. When this occurs, the impact of official intervention may be weakened or totally avoided (Hepburn, 1975:394-395; see also Hepburn, 1977:165-166).

Those investigations which have included the concept of significant others have consistently operationalized it only in terms of conforming others. The original, nondeviant referents of mother, father, and close personal friends have been used exclusively as that audience which evaluates and affects the self-evaluations of labeled deviants (Reckless et al., 1956, 1957; Burkett, 1972; Kaplan, 1976; Hepburn, 1977). While the response of these groups may be a necessary condition in deviance causation, the nature of interaction with noncomforming others may likewise be crucial. That is, deviant as well as nondeviant groups may serve as referents for identity and behavior. The neglect of the former in empirical investigations of labeling theory may account for the lack of support generated for the perspective.

Furthermore, the assumption that legitimate group response is a sufficient condition for deviant role-taking may not be applicable to many forms of deviance, insofar as deviant role models are not readily available in legitimate groups. In this situation, deviants have only to rely on the expectations of nondeviants as transmitted to them through interpersonal encounters or through official designation of their behavior as falling outside the limits of legitimate group requirements. Apart from the messages contained in these responses, and whatever individuals may already know of the cultural definitions of their situation, the person does not always have others to imitate, to model himself after in an attempt to establish a meaningful role as defined for him by the larger society. For this he must eventually shift reference associations from those who have labeled him and responded to him as deviant, to those who accept him as an equal and who have adopted similar roles for themselves as a result of like experiences in the community at large. In this manner, one becomes familiar with the nature of the role and, at the same time, acquires the knowledge, symbols, and support necessary for its enactment. This is an interpretive process based both on the responses encountered in the larger society and on the more intimate interaction within the deviant group.

In general, then, reference groups, with their values, beliefs, and attitudes, determine the standards by which individuals evelute themselves. As persons are identified as deviant by legitimate referents, they may shift to those groups more sympathetic to the deviant identity. The support provided by other deviants has obvious consequences for continued nonconformity. Accepted by a group which rewards individuals precisely because they are deviant, persons may become further committed to their deviant roles.

What few studies have included a measure of deviant association are encouraging. Labeled deviants do evaluate positively persons who represent their own marginal status (Chapman, 1966; Moriarity, 1974). In addition, subsequent behavior appears to be influenced by those sharing the deviant attribute (Moriarity, 1974; Ageton and Elliott, 1974; Farrell and Nelson, 1976). Such findings suggest that those individuals whose behavior has been called into question by more conforming groups may develop new attachments to others similarly disvalued. When this occurs, the organization of behavior and identity around the deviation may be virtually assured.

REFERENT OTHERS AND LABELING OUTCOMES

Theoretical developments within the labeling approach to deviant behavior are clear. The role of referent others in the deviance defining process, contrary to its treatment in labeling research, is multiple. Others not only apply labels, a role overemphasized in the research, but others also respond to individuals once the label has been applied. It is the nature of this latter response that will determine subsequent behavior on the part of those labeled.

Following public recognition of nonconformity, negotiations between labeled deviants and their significant others may result in one of several outcomes.[2] The original primary reference group may continue to accept the individual on the basis of the nondeviant identity. By refusing to recognize the legitimacy of external evaluations of the behavior of one of its members, primary others may fail to treat the nonconformer in terms of the expectations implied by the label. Examples of this pattern appear in earlier research. Many of the "good boys" studied by Reckless et al. (1956, 1957) did, in fact, have histories of contact with legal authorities. In spite of this, parents, teachers, and friends continued to think of the old juveniles as essentially good, as did the boys themselves. In like manner, parents of apprehended juveniles who, before the arrest, thought of their children as basically good, continued to believe so in spite of what happened with the police (Foster et al., 1972: 204). Farrell's (1972) investigation of homosexuals revealed again similar results. Most of the homosexuals studied indicated that they perceived continued acceptance from primary others. What rejection they did experience came from those with whom they were less intimately associated. Furthermore, persons who perceived rejection in public encounters were able to maintain positive self-definitions if they perceived acceptance from those with whom they were in primary group relations (Farrell, 1972:85-95, 99-101).

Given the nature of the interaction that characterizes primary and secondary associations, the above findings are not surprising. Contact within secondary groups usually involves limited knowledge of the other and is lacking the empathic role-taking dimension found in primary groups. As a result, persons will more often respond to labeled deviants in terms of the public definition of the behavior. When social conditions facilitate face-to-face interaction of extended duration, however, there is greater feedback from the individual and an eventual emergence of a shared definition of his situation (Farrell and Morrione, 1974:432). The continued acceptance of the nonconformer and non-legitimation of the label that ensue from such interaction thus render the behavioral consequences of public labeling ineffective. Deviation in this instance may be expected to remain at its primary level.

Alternatively, while significant others are reluctant to *reject* individuals, continued acceptance may be in terms of the imputed deviance. In this instance, the labeled nonconformer will not experience alienation from his original reference group but will find his deviant status validated by these associations. Such an outcome is similar to that described by Erikson in his study of schizophrenia in the military (Dentler and Erikson, 1959). Army recruits resisted elimination of preinstitutionalized psychotics from their training units. While recognizing that the nonconformer was not capable of performing daily army routines, the groups erected protective shells around such persons lest military authorities become aware of the deviant's behavior. Similarly, wives of psychotic spouses have also been found to exert great effort in maintaining the original relationship. Definitions of the bizarre behavior as in need of institutional intervention were denied as long as accommodation within the family could be maintained (Schwartz, 1957). Finally, in a study of perceptions of stigma among apprehended juveniles, youths did not appear to perceive any loss of esteem among significant others. Upon closer inspection, however, it was found that among the parents sampled were those who already regarded their sons as prone to trouble and who expressed no surprise, therefore, at the latest delinquent encounter (Foster et al., 1972:204). Here, even though the children had been officially designated deviant, there was no subsequent change in parental reaction. In sum, it is argued that when the response of significant others involves acceptance of the deviance, the labeled individual will tend toward an intensification of and commitment to the behavior. In this instance, the support of primary others is seen as instrumental in propelling the individual toward a pattern of secondary deviation.

The third possible response of primary groups is, of course, to reject the labeled deviant. It is this course of action that is implied in most labeling research. On the basis of this rejection, it is further presumed that additional deviant behavior will ensue. Commitment to nonconformity following primary group rejection, however, is itself problematic.

Given the individual's need for associations conducive to the maintenance of a positive self-concept (Chapman, 1966), rejection by one's original reference group may be stress producing (Parsons, 1951; Cohen, 1955, 1959) and may generate, therefore, the need to adapt. Such adaptation may involve selection of a new reference group. The response of this group to the labeled deviant is itself variable.

In one instance, the adopted referent others may accept the nonconformer on a nondeviant basis. This is the purpose, for example, of such group support organizations as Weight Watchers and Alcoholics Anonymous. While maintaining that the essential identity of their members remains forever "fat" or "alcoholic," the effort is to convert discrediting stigma into discreditable stigma (Goffman, 1963; Laslett and Warren, 1975; Warren, 1974; Roman and Trice, 1968; Trice and Roman, 1970). Drug rehabilitation programs, religious organizations, as well as more informal associations perform a similar function. By relating to the deviant on the basis of a more legitimate status, such groups may prevent reorganization of the individual's life and identity around continued deviation.

Rejected by the original primary others, individuals may also develop associations with those whose acceptance is in terms of the deviant label. This subcultural adaptation (Cohen, 1955, 1959) involves the interaction of individuals who share similar problems of adjustment to the stigmatizing label and who, through their interaction, can offer each of the members a more positive evaluation of the deviant role.

Nature of Group Acceptance	Nature of Referent Identification-Association	
	Identification-Association with Original Group	Identification-Association with Adopted Group
Acceptance as Non-deviant	Primary deviance	Primary deviance
Acceptance as Deviant	Secondary deviance	Secondary deviance

Figure 1: BEHAVIORAL CONSEQUENCES OF THE NATURE OF REFERENT IDENTIFICATION-ASSOCIATION AND GROUP ACCEPTANCE

The concept of subcultural association has long occupied an important position in explorations of deviant behavior. Its utilization in labeling research, however, has been limited. The evidence that is available indicates that enculturation of labeled nonconformers to deviant subcultures may follow perceived societal rejection (Farrell and Nelson, 1976). If individuals perceive rejection from legitimate society, they may adapt to the stigma by shifting reference associations to deviant groups. While providing collective support, the ultimate outcome of these associations may be further identification with the deviant role and the eventual development of secondary deviation.

The varying response patterns of significant others to designated deviance and the implications of such responses for future behavior are illustrated in Figure 1.

CONCLUSION

It has been the thesis of this paper that the labeling approach to social deviance is characterized by a research tradition that has abandoned its link with the theory and antecedent developments in symbolic interactionism. The interactionist perspective includes as its most basic assumption the notion of referent identification and association. It is through the ongoing processes of such communicative interaction that symbolic realities are constructed and reconstructed. In this manner, individuals come to attach meaning to the behaviors of self and others. Such a premise lies so close to the heart of the interactionist perspective as to have become a "taken for granted" assumption within the approach.

Labeling research, however, while positing the importance of the reactions of others in the development of deviant careers, has overlooked the role of referent identifications and associations in this process. The question has been raised, therefore, concerning whether the failure to generate empirical support for the theory lies in the absence of these concepts as explanatory variables. We have argued that the problem of deviant and nondeviant adaptations to labeling concerns the several patterns of interaction with those whose acceptance of deviant attributes and behaviors are themselves variable.

NOTES

1. Meade (1974) points out, however, that his own positive findings are only suggestive of the labeling hypothesis. Without an analysis of the subjective states of sanctioned individuals, alternative explanations of the original relationship remain unchallenged. Those persons eventually labeled may in fact be more committed to lives of deviance. Such a possibility constitutes an equally plausible explanation of the available supportive evidence. Until it and similar competing hypotheses can be eliminated, labeling theory remains untested.

2. To be sure, the labeling of an individual as deviant involves more than the application of formal sanctions. Informal labeling and self-labeling are equally important concepts and may in fact precede official designations. Given the emphasis on formal labeling in the literature, and for reasons of space, the discussion is limited to those instances where public recognition of nonconformity precedes the responses of significant others.

REFERENCES

AGETON, S.S. and ELLIOTT, D.S. (1974). "The effects of legal processing on delinquent orientations." Social Problems 22:87-100.

BECKER, H.S. (1963). Outsiders. New York: Free Press.

BURGESS, R.L. and AKERS, R.L. (1968). "A differential association-reinforcement theory of criminal behavior." Social Problems 14:128-147.

BURKETT, S.R. (1972). "Self-other systems and deviant career patterns: The small group situation." Pacific Sociological Review 15: 169-183.

CAMERON, M.O. (1964). The booster and the snitch: Department store shoplifting. New York: Free Press.

CHAMBLISS, W.J. and LIELL, J.T. (1966). "The legal process in the community setting: A study of law enforcement." Crime and Delinquency 12:310-317.

CHAPMAN, I. (1966). "Race and self-concept of delinquents and nondelinquents." Sociological Quarterly 7:373-379.

COHEN, A.C. (1955). Delinquent boys. New York: Free Press.

——— (1959). "The study of social disorganization and deviant behavior." Pp. 461-484 in R.K. Merton, L. Broom, and L.S. Cottrell (eds.), Sociology today. New York: Basic Books.

COOLEY, C.H. (1902). Human nature and the social order. New York: Scribner's.

DeLAMATER, J. (1968). "On the nature of deviance." Social Forces 46:445-455.

DENTLER, R.A. and ERIKSON, K.T. (1959). "The functions of deviance in groups." Social Problems 7:98-107.

ERICSON, R.V. (1977). "Social distance and reaction to criminality." British Journal of Criminology 17:16-29.

FARRELL, R.A. (1972). "Societal reaction to homosexuals: Toward a generalized theory of deviance." Ph.D. dissertation, University of Cincinnati.

FARRELL, R.A. and MORRIONE, T.J. (1974). "Social interaction and stereotypic responses to homosexuals." Archives of Sexual Behavior 3:425-442.

——— (1975). "Conforming to deviance." Pp. 375-387 in R.A. Farrell and V.L. Swigert (eds.), Social deviance. Philadelphia: J.P. Lippincott.

FARRELL, R.A. and NELSON, J.F. (1976). "A causal model of secondary deviance: The case of homosexuality." Sociological Quarterly 17:109-120.

FARRINGTON, D.P. (1977). "The effects of public labelling." British Journal of Criminology 17:112-125.

FISHER, S. (1972). "Stigma and deviant careers in school." Social Problems 20:78-83.

FOSTER, J.D., DINITZ, S., and RECKLESS, W.C. (1972). "Perceptions of stigma following public intervention for delinquent behavior." Social Problems 20:202-209.

GIBBS, J.P. (1962). "Rates of mental hospitalization: A study of societal reaction to deviant behavior." American Sociological Review 27:782-792.

GLASER, D. (1956). "Criminality theories and behavioral images." American Journal of Sociology 61:433-444.

GOFFMAN, E. (1963). Stigma: Notes on the management of spoiled identity. Englewood Cliffs, N.J.: Prentice-Hall.

GOLD, M. and WILLIAMS, J.R. (1969). "National study of the aftermath of apprehension." Prospectus 3:3-12.

GOLDMAN, N. (1963). The differential selection of juvenile offenders for court appearance. New York: National Research and Information Center, National Council on Crime and Delinquency.

HEPBURN, J.R. (1975). "The role of the audience in deviant behavior and deviant identity." Sociology and Social Research 59:387-405.

——— (1977). "Official deviance and spoiled identity: Delinquents and their significant others." Pacific Sociological Review 20:163-179.

KAPLAN, H. (1976). "Self attitudes and deviant response." Social Forces 54:788-801.

KLEIN, M.W. (1974). "Labeling, deterrence, and recidivism: A study of police dispositions of juvenile offenders." Social Problems 22:292-303.

LARKIN, W. and LOMAN, L.A. (1977). "Labeling in the family context: An experimental study." Sociology and Social Research 61:192-203.

LASLETT, B. and WARREN, C.A. (1975). "Losing weight: The organizational promotion of a behavior change." Social Problems 23:69-80.

LEMERT, E.M. (1951). Social pathology: A systematic approach to the theory of sociopathic behavior. New York: McGraw-Hill.

——— (1962). "Stuttering and social structure in two Pacific Island societies." Journal of Speech and Hearing Disorders 27:3-10.

LOMAN, L.A. and LARKIN, W.E. (1976). "Rejection of the mentally ill: An experiment in labeling." Sociological Quarterly 17:555-560.

MEAD, G.H. (1934). Mind, self and society. Chicago: University of Chicago Press.

MEADE, A.C. (1974). "The labeling approach to delinquency: State of the theory as a function of method." Social Forces 53:83-91.

MECHANIC, D. (1962). "Some factors in identifying and defining mental illness." Mental Hygiene 46:66-74.

MORIARTY, T. (1974). "Role of stigma in the experience of deviance." Journal of Personality and Social Psychology 29:849-855.

PARSONS, T. (1951). The social system. New York: Free Press.

PHILLIPS, D.L. (1963). "Rejection: A possible consequence of seeking help for mental disorders." American Sociological Review 28:963-972.

RECKLESS, W.C., DINITZ, S., and MURRAY, E. (1956). "Self concept as an insulator against delinquency." American Sociological Review 21:744-746.

——— (1957). "The 'good' boy in a high delinquency area." Journal of Criminal Law, Criminology and Police Science 48:18-26.

REED, J.P. and REED, R.S. (1973). "Status, images, and consequence: Once a criminal always a criminal." Sociology and Social Research 57:460-472.

ROMAN, P.M. and TRICE, H.M. (1968). "The sick role, labeling theory and the deviant drinker." International Journal of Social Psychiatry 14:245-251.

SCHEFF, T.J. (1966). Being Mentally Ill. Chicago: Aldine.

SCHUR, E.M. (1971). Labeling Deviant Behavior: Its Sociological Implications. New York: Harper and Row.

SCHWARTZ, C. (1957). "Perspectives on deviance—wives' definitions of their husbands' mental illness." Psychiatry 20:275-291.

SCHWARTZ, R.D. and SKOLNICK, J.H. (1962). "Two studies of legal stigma." Social Problems 10:133-142.

SCOTT, R.A. (1969). The Making of Blind Men. New York: Russell Sage.

SHOEMAKER, D.J., SOUTH, D.R., and LOWE, J. (1973). "Facial stereotypes of deviants and judgements of guilt or innocence." Social Forces 51:427-433.

SIMMONS, J.L. (1965). "Public stereotypes of deviants." Social Problems 13: 223-232.

SKOLNICK, J.H. (1966). Justice without trial: Law enforcement in democratic society. New York: John Wiley.

STINCHCOMBE, A.J. (1963). "Institutions of privacy in the determination of police administrative practice." American Journal of Sociology 69:150-159.

SUTHERLAND, E. (1947). Principles of criminology. Philadelphia: J.P. Lippincott.

SWIGERT, V.L. and FARRELL, R.A. (1976). Murder, inequality and the law. Lexington, Mass.: D.C. Heath.

——— (1977). "Normal homicides and the law." American Sociological Review 42:16-32.

TANNENBAUM, F. (1938). Crime and the community. New York: Columbia University Press.

TRICE, H.M. and ROMAN, P.M. (1970). "Delabeling, relabeling, and Alcoholics Anonymous." Social Problems 17:538-546.

WARREN, C.A.B. (1974). "The use of stigmatizing social labels in conventionalizing deviant behavior." Sociology and Social Research 58:303-311.

WEINBERG, M.S. (1966). "Becoming a nudist." Psychiatry 29:15-24.

WILLIAMS, C. and WEINBERG, M.S. (1971). Homosexuals and the military. New York: Harper & Row.

Charles W. Thomas
Bowling Green State
University

Jeffrey M. Hyman
University of Guam

5

COMPLIANCE THEORY, CONTROL THEORY, AND JUVENILE DELINQUENCY

Although schools are expected to prepare students for adult social and vocational roles, a variety of studies suggest that they may inadvertently stimulate delinquent behavior. Some emphasize the status frustration experienced by students from disadvantaged backgrounds (Cohen, 1955; Elliott, 1966). Others devote attention to the positions students hold within the school status hierarchy (Kvaraceus, 1945; Reiss and Rhodes, 1961; Sexton, 1961; Gold, 1963, 1970; Kelly and Balch, 1971; Kelly, 1971, 1972). Still others underline the importance of the bonds between students and their school (Hirschi, 1969; Hindelang, 1973; Thomas et al., 1977).

The common denominator is that school experiences have a significant relationship with delinquency. The nature of this relationship remains unclear, however, and much

AUTHORS' NOTE: This is a revised version of a paper presented to the annual meeting of the American Society of Criminology, Atlanta, Georgia, 1977. The authors are grateful for the assistance of Susan Enea and Marcia Isbell, both of whom are members of the Department of Sociology at Bowling Green State University. This research was supported by two grants from the National Institute for Juvenile Justice and Delinquency Prevention, #75-NI-99-0031 and #76-NI-99-0050. This financial support, however, does not necessarily indicate the concurrence of NIJJDP in any of the statements or conclusions presented here.

of the ambiguity may be a consequence of the superficial attention given to the organizational aspects of public schools. Organizational theory and research have not emphasized delinquency (Bidwell, 1965; Corwin, 1970, 1974; Willower et al., 1967; Helsel and Willower, 1974; Newton, 1975); delinquency research has generally concentrated on only such specific organizational attributes as curriculum tracking (Stinchcombe, 1964; Hargreaves, 1968; Schafer et al., 1970; Schafer and Olexa, 1971) and school-imposed sanctions (Vinter and Sarri, 1965; Thomas, 1977). Consequently, we know little about the effect of school organizations on the attitudes and behavior of juveniles.

One of the points at which we might begin to attack this shortcoming has been detailed by Etzioni (1975) and other students of compliance theory. All would stipulate that social control is a salient problem for public schools. Attaining and maintaining some minimum level of control is an obvious prerequisite for success in other areas, but the methods employed in serving this goal can have negative consequences (Etzioni, 1975; Thomas et al., 1977). When control is problematic, coercive power is often employed to insure compliance. The exercise of coercion, however, can yield alienative involvement, and the negative commitment which is associated with such alienation can weaken or break bonds that might otherwise exist between students and the organization of which they are a part. Hirschi (1969) and others (Hindelang, 1973; Thomas et al., 1977) have argued that the weakening of these bonds increases the likelihood of delinquency.

Although this reasoning rests on sound theoretical premises, its empirical adequacy has not been established. Thus, the purpose of this study will be to assess the importance of student perceptions of the power employed by school organizations. The basic hypothesis is that students may become alienatively involved in the school because of their negative evaluations of the power exercised in attaining control goals. Should this happen, control theory suggests that it may weaken attachment to both the school and the conventional society which the school represents. This, in turn, may result in increased delinquency. Further, the analysis is designed in such a way that the importance of attachment to school relative to the importance of other dimensions of control theory may be assessed.

THEORETICAL ORIENTATION

The theoretical problem we confront is relatively simple. Etzioni's (1975) statement of compliance theory emphasizes the relationship between the type of power employed by an organization as a means of insuring the compliance of organizational participants and the type of involvement those participants will have in the organization. By itself, however, compliance theory does not provide an explanation of juvenile delinquency. Control theory, on the other hand, tells us comparatively little about how the bonds to an organization can be broken, but it devotes a good deal of attention to how weakened or broken bonds affect delinquency. To the extent that the two models can be brought together, one would expect that our ability to understand some aspects of delinquency would be enhanced. Thus, an overview of compliance and control theory is appropriate.

First of all, Etzioni (1975:3) defines compliance as "a relation in which an actor behaves in accordance with a directive supported by another actor's power, and to the orientation of the subordinated actor to the power applied." Compliance consists of both a structural and motivational component. The structural component refers to the power allocated to one group of actors as a means of bringing about the compliance of those subordinate to them: Three basic types of power are delineated: *coercive power,* which refers to the actual or potential application of physical sanctions; *remunerative power,* which reflects the manipulation of such material rewards as salaries, wages, or services; and *normative power,* which involves the utilization of such symbolic rewards as the granting or withdrawal of esteem and prestige. The motivational aspect refers to the orientation, involvement, or commitment of those subject to the power which is exercised. Etzioni contends that reliance on coercive power most commonly produces *alienative involvement* (an intense negative orientation toward the organization); that remunerative power yields *calculative involvement* (either a positive or a negative orientation of low intensity); and that normative power tends to evoke *moral involvement* (an intensely positive orientation).

While these relationships between power and involvement are viewed as the most common ones we are likely to encounter, Etzioni (1975:45-67) does not ignore the possibility of other combinations. Indeed, he (1975:45) contends that "educational organizations characteristically employ normative controls, with coercion as a secondary source of compliance. . . . Coercion has declined in significance over the last decades, for modern education de-emphasizes 'discipline' as a goal and stresses internalization of norms." While this view may apply to higher education, we do not agree that it is appropriate in most secondary schools. To the contrary, our contention is that the reverse is far more often the case. Public schools would prefer to rely on normative controls, but they are commonly unable to do so for a variety of reasons. Not the least of these are the inability of schools to assume commitment to their goals on the part of those entering the organization, the obvious difficulties involved in establishing any recruitment and selection standards, and the absence of any effective means by which students who fail to conform to organizational directives may be removed (Bidwell, 1965; Brim and Wheeler, 1966; Etzioni, 1975:261-264). Further, despite much contemporary concern with the attainment of such organizational goals as technical socialization, the difficulty of quantifying these goals and the immediacy of social control problems often have the consequence of schools being evaluated and evaluating themselves in terms of how effectively they maintain social control. For example, we are all familiar with the administrative point of view which holds that a teacher who is able to control his or her students is, by definition, a good teacher. In other words, what should be viewed as a means of pursuing other goals (controlling students) is very often translated into a goal itself.

In short, our contention is that public schools are being called upon to accept large numbers of students whose commitment to the goals of the organization is not the logical outcome of self-selection, the implementation of recruitment standards, or the utilization of meaningful removal standards. Consequently, social control can be and often is so problematic that it becomes a major organizational goal, a goal that is commonly pursued by a primary reliance on coercive power and a secondary reliance on normative power. The anticipated outcome is that large numbers of students will become alienatively involved.

This is the point at which control theory assumes special importance. It is far more concerned with the relationships between students, school experience, and delinquency than is compliance theory. This stems in part from the basic issue posed by control theory: ''The question is, 'Why don't we do it?' There is much evidence that we would if we dared'' (Hirschi, 1969:34). For our purposes, the answer to Hirschi's question is straightforward. Students are less likely to engage in delinquency when their bonds to conventionality are strengthened by their positive commitment to or involvement in school, but that bond is often weakened as an unintended result of efforts to insure social control.

Control theory, of course, is more complex than this discussion implies. It would be incorrect to suggest that control theorists view school experiences as the only variables which are of significance in the study of juvenile delinquency. To the contrary, Hirschi (1969:16-34) contends that a juvenile's bond to conventionality is composed of at least four interrelated elements: attachment, commitment, involvement, and belief. *Attachment* may be defined as the respect accorded the expectations and opinions of others; *commitment* refers to one's investment or stake in conventional activities; *involvement* is linked to the proportion of one's time which is consumed by conventional behavior; and *belief* refers to the adoption of values which define unconventional behavior as inappropriate. While school experiences impact on bonds to the conventional society, they in no way exhaust the sources of intensified or weakened bonds. Nevertheless, the general expectation advanced here is that students may view themselves as being powerless participants in their schools as a consequence of the efforts made by school officials to insure social control, that the alienation which this reflects will weaken the bond between students and the school, and that this weakened bond will be associated with delinquency involvement.

RESEARCH METHODOLOGY

The data presented here were collected from public school students in Portsmouth and Virginia Beach, Virginia, during the 1975-1976 school year. A cluster sampling design was employed, within which the basic sampling unit was classes. Two classes were randomly selected from each grade level at all of the junior and senior high schools in both cities. The classes were selected from those required of all students. The data were obtained by means of a self-administered questionnaire at both the beginning and end of the school year, and complete questionnaires were obtained on 2,249 students at both points in time. Stated somewhat differently, we were able to obtain data at both points in time from 74.3% of the sample of students in grades 8-12.

An overview of the social and demographic characteristics of this sample may prove useful. Responses to the initial questionnaire show that 74.3% of the students were white, 47.2% were male, and 39.9% were sixteen years old or older. With respect to the grade level distribution, 42.5% were in grades 8 or 9 and 56.6% were in grades 10-12. Some 31.3% were enrolled in college preparatory classes, 9.8% were taking business courses, 6.2% reported taking vocational training courses, and the majority, 51.0%, were enrolled in a general curriculum. The distribution on a seven-point occupational prestige measure shows that those in the sample tended to come from somewhat higher socioeconomic categories than might be found in some areas. For example, only 6.9% were placed in the two lowest categories on the scale. This, however, is clearly a reflection of the affluent status of many of the families in the Virginia Beach segment of our sample.

The operational measures of the major independent and dependent variables are described below, and each of the attitudinal measures may be obtained from the authors.

Alienation. Both Etzioni (1975) and Hirschi (1969) define attachment in general terms. Neither identify the specific aspects of the school which students may negatively evaluate. It is possible, however, to divide the attachment concept into more manageable components, one of which is alienation from school. The measure of alienation employed here combines Etzioni's (1975) and Seeman's (1959) definitions of the term. Whereas Seeman refers to alienation as resulting from general structural conditions, Etzioni directs attention toward the consequences of specific organizations within which people participate. The primary focus here is on the powerlessness dimension of alienation, which is viewed as structurally specific. It is proposed that the greater the reliance on coercive power by an organization, the lower the personal control allowed lower participants. Students who evaluate the school as coercive should perceive the organization as depriving them of a significant degree of decision-making power with regard to organizational policies, rules, and regulations.

In addition to examining students' assessment of the personal control exercised in school, consideration is given to whether they view it as a salient concern. The contention is that because they spend only a portion of each day in school they may not evaluate a lack of control within this particular setting as dissatisfying. Attention must focus on whether feelings of powerlessness represent a frustrating condition. Thus, alienation is conceptualized as a product of perceptions of powerlessness and the saliency of these perceptions. As with the remaining variables, Likert-type attitude scales were used. All of the scales were developed with data collected in the fall. The total pool of items designed to measure the attitude under consideration was factor analyzed. Only those items having a factor loading of .30 or greater on the first factor of the unrotated factor matrix were included in the final scale. The powerlessness and saliency scales were factor analyzed separately. Scores on the final alienation measure were set equal to the product of their scores on the two measures. The scale has a mean of 184.95 and a standard deviation of 81.44. The higher the scale score on this measure, the greater the alienation.

Attachment to the School Organization. Another component of the attachment concept is student affect toward the school organization. This measure reflects general attitudes toward the school and the way it is run. Those who perceive the institution as coercive are expected to express negative attitudes on this dimension. The six items that comprise this scale have a mean of 14.95 and a standard deviation of 4.62. High scores on this scale are indicative of negative attachment to the school organization.

Attachment to School Involvement. A third aspect of attachment is student attitudes toward involvement in school. The theoretical model noted that the need for coercive power arises partly because students are often involuntary participants in the organization. The application of coercive power and, more important, student perceptions of the power which is employed, may promote a negative orientation toward school involvement. The measure used here evaluates the degree to which students view participation in school as nonrewarding. This scale consists of six items. It has a mean of 14.23 and a standard deviation of 4.52. The higher the scale score, the more negative the affect toward school involvement.

Evaluations of Organizational Effectiveness. A final dimension of attachment is evaluations of the effectiveness

of the school. As with other "people-processing organizations" (Brim and Wheeler, 1966), schools are established
to effect changes in those they process. However, to the
extent that social order within school is problematic and
students negatively evaluate the means used to secure
social control, they are unlikely to see any long-term benefits deriving from their participation. Instead, they will view
the school as ineffective. The variable used here measures
whether students view the school as helping them to think
clearly, make them better persons, and provide skills required for future occupational roles. Six items are included
in the scale. The mean of the measure is 13.78, with a
standard deviation of 4.16. High-scale scores are associated
with negative evaluations of the effectiveness of the organization.

Attitudes toward the Law. Research has not examined
the importance of orientations to school in explaining delinquency relative to the effects of other bonding variables.
One variable which seems particularly important is a belief
in the moral validity of the law. Hirschi (1969:198) states
that "delinquency is not caused by beliefs that require
delinquency but is rather made possible by the absence of
(effective) beliefs that forbid delinquency." This variable is
measured with a six-item scale, and it assesses the degree
to which students view the law as morally binding. The
scale has a mean of 13.03 and a standard deviation of 3.96.
High scores mean that students do not feel bound by societal expectations.

Educational Expectations. Hirschi (1969:162) notes that
individuals who are committed to conventional goals or
lines of action are unlikely to commit delinquent acts, since
"rather than being a means of realizing conventional
aspirations," delinquency is, if anything, "a means of pre-
cluding their attainment." Students' educational expectations provide one measure of their commitment to conventional goals. This variable is measured through responses
to the question, "Do you plan on going to college?" This
item has five response categories which represent degrees

of certainty regarding college plans. Scores on this and the remaining bonding variables are based on data gathered in the fall. The mean for this measure is 2.19, with a standard deviation of 1.12. The higher the score, the lower students' educational expectations.

Involvement in Conventional Activities. Another element of the bond to the larger society is involvement in conventional activities. The more individuals are engrossed in such activities, the less time they will have for participation in deviant behavior. A six-item index is employed in operationalizing this variable. The six items include the number of hours students spend each week with their family, on extracurricular activities not related to the school, on church activities, in community activities with friends, working on a job, and in social activities with people their age. This measure has a mean of 16.85 and a standard deviation of 2.77. The higher the score, the less the time spent each week on these activities.

Involvement in School-Related Activities. The involvement dimension of the conventional bond is also measured with reference to participation in school-related activities. This index includes the amount of time students devote each week to homework and school athletics, and it is scored in the same fashion as the preceding measure. The mean for this index is 6.38, with a standard deviation of 1.37.

Juvenile Delinquency. The major dependent variable of the study is delinquency. This variable was measured through responses to a series of self-report items. The following weighting scheme was applied to the offenses: petty theft, purchasing of alcohol, truancy, and use of a false identification were assigned a weight of one; running away from home, fighting, theft of an object valued between $2 and $50, destruction of public or private property, and joyriding were given a weight of two; and use of a weapon, breaking into a house, store, or office, auto theft, and theft of an object valued at more than $50 were assigned a weight of four. Each student indicated the number of times they committed the acts during the 1975-1976 school year. The frequencies were scored in the following manner: never was assigned a score of zero; one through seven times was set equal to the number of times committed; and eight or more times was given a value of eight. A delinquency score for each student was obtained by multiplying the seriousness weights by the frequency scores for all offenses and summing the products.

An effort was made to arrange the independent and dependent variables temporarily. The bonding variables were measured with the data collected in the fall; the scores for the delinquency scale were computed from responses to the spring questionnaire.

The measure has a mean of 3.59 and a standard deviation of 5.49. The higher the score, the greater the degree of delinquency involvement.

ANALYSIS AND FINDINGS

Hirschi (1969) suggests that the bonds to conventional society are interrelated and that all are determinants of juvenile delinquency. If this is so, then associations should emerge between the attachment measures, the two involvement indices, educational expectations, the law scale, and the spring delinquency measure. The information necessary to evaluate the proposed relationships is presented in Table 1.

The zero-order correlations provide partial support for the assertion that elements of the bond to conventional society are interrelated. While the two involvement indices are moderately related to each other (r = .229), they have weak correlations with almost all of the other measures of conventional bonds. The exceptions to this are the moderate relationships between involvement in school activities and attachment to school involvement (r = .292), educational expectations (r = .267), and evaluations of the effectiveness of the school organization (r = .225). The remaining control theory variables are more supportive of the prediction that a loosening of one type of bond is accompanied

Table 1: Zero-Order Correlations Between Alienation (X1), Attachment to School Involvement (X3), Evaluations of Organizational Effectiveness (X4), Attitudes Toward the Law (X5), Educational Expectations (X6), Extra-School Conventional Activities (X7), School-Related Activities (X8), and Juvenile Delinquency (X9)

	X1	X2	X3	X4	X5	X6	X7	X8	X9
X1	1.000	.591	.383	.461	.286	.105	.038*	.081	.198
X2		1.000	.646	.643	.382	.237	.100	.177	.262
X3			1.000	.588	.393	.360	.153*	.292	.232
X4				1.000	.411	.126	.058*	.026	.197
X5					1.000	.213	.068	.147	.333
X6						1.000	.110	.267	.163
X7							1.000	.229	−.004*
X8								1.000	−.038
X9									1.000

by a weakening of others. With the exception of the low correlation between educational expectations and contextual alienation (r = .105), the attachment measures, the commitment variable, and the law scale are moderately to strongly related to one another.

As was noted above, control theory predicts that delinquency is possible when an individual's link to the conventional society has been broken. Although Table 1 does not furnish all of the information needed to address this issue, the correlations show that the control theory variables have weak to moderate correlations with the spring delinquency measure, the law scale being most strongly related to the dependent variable (r = .333). Similarly, both attachment to the school organization and school involvement are moderately related to self-reported delinquency (r = .262 and .232, respectively). However, the measures of alienation from the school, evaluations of organizational effectiveness, and college plans have relatively weak correlations with delinquency involvement (r = .198, .197, .163, respectively). Further, the correlation between student involvement in school activities and the dependent variable is substantively trivial (r = .038). Similarly, the index of involvement in conventional activities outside of school has an insignificant relationship with the spring delinquency measure (r = .004).

In short, the findings reported here provide only partial support for the basic hypotheses of control theory. Further, the correlations do not reveal either the total amount of variance in delinquency explained by this set of measures or the importance of school attachment measures relative to that of the other components of control theory. To address these issues we relied on multiple regression analysis. Only those variables which yielded regression coefficients that were significant at the .001 level in the preliminary regression analysis were retained in the final multiple regression equations.

Our initial attention focused on the explanatory power of the four attachment variables. As has already been noted, each of these variables has significant correlations with delinquency, but all are both rather strongly correlated with one another and weakly correlated with juvenile delinquency. Consequently, the expectation is that the proportion of variance in delinquency which can be explained by these variables will not be as strong as originally predicted. That is exactly what we found. Although attachment to the school organization, attachment to school involvement, and alienation produced significant regression coefficients, the measure of perceived organizational effectiveness did not. In addition, the multiple correlation coefficient of .307 shows that the three significant predictor variables explain only 9.4% of the variance in delinquency. In short, the school attachment variables, while obviously of some importance, do not play nearly so important a role as had been anticipated.

In moving beyond this aspect of the analysis we encounter a more complex problem. The fact that the attachment measures were intercorrelated with one another posed no problems for the first segment of the multiple regression analysis, largely because we did not wish to rank the four variables in terms of their relative importance. Now, however, we need to incorporate the additional influence of our measures of the commitment, involvement, and belief dimensions of control theory. In doing so, we need to determine the relative importance of each of the four dimensions. The problem is that these variables are sufficiently intercorrelated that the standardized regression coefficients cannot be expected to provide an unambiguous estimate of the relative importance of each variable (e.g., Blalock, 1963; Farrar and Glauber, 1967; Gordon, 1968). One way to resolve this problem is to compute a series of regression equations employing the same set of predictor variables. Each will produce the same set of regression coefficients and the same multiple correlation coefficient. By forcing each dimension of bonds to conventionality into an equation on the last step of a stepwise solution, however, we can obtain a measure of the unique contribution which each makes to the explained variance in the dependent variable. The attachment, belief, commitment, and involvement aspects of control theory may then be ordered in terms of their explanatory power as determined by the magnitude of their unique contributions (Kerlinger and Pedhauzer, 1973:297-298).

The obvious result of incorporating the additional control theory variables is that the multiple correlation increases from the .307 obtained with only the attachment variables to .415. In other words, the entire set of variables is able to explain 17.2% of the variance in delinquency. Further, all of this variance is attributable to the influence of the attachment, belief, and commitment variables. As might be expected from the near-zero correlations between the two measures of involvement and delinquency shown in Table 1, involvement in school-related and other types of activities produced insignificant regression coefficients and, therefore, were deleted from the analysis. Equally important, however, are the findings regarding the relative importance of the attachment, belief, and commitment variables. The belief dimension of control theory, as measured here by attitudes toward the law, is clearly the most important influence. Even when it was forced into the regression equation on the last step, it still produced a 7.3% increase in the explained variance. The attachment variables were the second most important influence. That set of variables added 2.6% to the explained variance when forced into the equation or the last step of the computations. Finally, while statistically significant, the commitment aspect of control theory, as reflected here by the educational expectations variable, was the least important influence.

DISCUSSION

It is difficult to interpret the results of the analysis. Taken by itself, it is obvious that our ability to account for only a bit more than 17% of the variance in juvenile delinquency when we employ the entire set of control theory variables should not lead us to place too much confidence in that perspective. On the other hand, it is very difficult to place these findings into an appropriate comparative context. For example, the most extensive investigations of control theory rely primarily on bivariate tabular analysis (Hirschi, 1969; Hindelang, 1973). Thus, there is no way to determine how much of the variance in delinquency these earlier studies were able to explain. About the best we can say is that the explained variance reported here is quite comparable to that reported in the relatively small number of studies which have reported multiple correlations (Thomas et al., 1977).

Viewed from a somewhat more positive angle, the results reported here have several implications for delinquency theory. Perhaps the most important of these is linked to our contention that there is an important overlap between the assertions of compliance and control theory. The former model directs our attention toward some of the factors which, in effect, can weaken the bond between students and schools; the latter perspective, while not as useful in accounting for how bonds may be weakened, does emphasize the link between weakened bonds and juvenile delinquency. The measures of attachment to school employed in this study, all of which are closely associated with compliance theory, do appear to play a sufficiently significant role that some further integration of compliance and control theory propositions might prove useful.

Second, Hirschi (1969) places a good deal of emphasis on the interrelationship between the components of control theory and on their independent effects. Although this point of view finds some support, the case is not nearly so clearcut as some have assumed. The measures of involvement used in this study, for example, proved almost useless, and their associations with other elements of control theory were far from strong. Similarly, our measure of commitment, while not an especially good one, did not play more than a very minor role in explaining delinquency.

Overall, however, this analysis provides at least partial support for many of the propositions which may be derived from control theory, and that support is certainly strengthened by the fact that the longitudinal aspect of our research design allows us to determine the temporal ordering of the variables much more precisely than has been the case in most previous research. Specifically, those students whose bonds to conventionality were negative at the beginning of the 1975-1976 school year, reported more involvement in delinquency during that year than did those with a more positive attachment to school, a greater commitment to conventional goals, and a more positive regard for the law. Thus, while control theory does not appear to provide anything close to a full explanation, its ability to account for a significant proportion of delinquency cannot be ignored.

REFERENCES

BIDWELL, C. (1965). "The school as a formal organization." Pp. 972-1020 in J. March (ed.), Handbook of organizations. Chicago: Rand McNally.
BLALOCK, H. (1963). "Correlated independent variables: The problem of multicollinearity." Social Forces 42 (December):233-237.
BRIM, O. and WHEELER, S. (1966). Socialization after childhood. New York: John Wiley.
COHEN, A. (1955). Delinquent boys: The culture of the gang. New York: Free Press.
CORWIN, R. (1970). Militant processionalism: A study of organizational conflict in high schools. New York: Appleton-Century-Crofts.
——— (1974). Education in crisis: A sociological analysis of schools and universities in transition. New York: John Wiley.
ELLIOTT, D. (1966). "Delinquency, school attendance and dropout." Social Problems 13 (Winter):307-324.
ETZIONI, A. (1975). A comparative analysis of complex organizations. New York: Free Press.
FARRARR, D. and GLAUBER, R. (1967). "Multicollinearity in regression analysis: The problem revisited." Review of Economics and Statistics 49 (February):92-107.
GOLD, M. (1963). Status forces in delinquent boys. Ann Arbor: University of Michigan Press.
——— (1970). Delinquent behavior in an American city. Belmont, Calif.: Wadsworth.
GORDON, R. (1968). "Issues in multiple regression." American Journal of Sociology 73 (March):592-616.

HARGREAVES, D. (1968). Social relations in a secondary school. New York: Humanities Press.

HELSEL, A. and WILLOWER, D. (1974). "Toward definition and measurement of pupil control behavior." Journal of Educational Administration 12 (May):114-123.

HINDELANG, M. (1973). "Causes of delinquency: A partial replication and extension." Social Problems 20 (Spring):417-487.

HIRSCHI, T. (1969). Causes of delinquency. Berkeley: University of California Press.

KELLY, D. (1971). "School failure, academic self-evaluation, and school avoidance and deviant behavior." Youth and Society 2 (June):489-503.

——— (1972). "Social origins and adolescent success patterns." Education and Urban Society 4 (May):351-365.

KELLY, D. and BALCH, R. (1971). "Social origins and school failure: A reexamination of Cohen's theory of working-class delinquency." Pacific Sociological Review 14 (October):413-430.

KERLINGER, F. and PEDHAUZER, E. (1973). Multiple regression in behavioral research. New York: Holt, Rinehart & Winston.

KVARACEUS, W. (1945). Juvenile delinquency and the school. New York: World Book Co.

NEWTON, E. (1975). "School organization in a changing society." Journal of Educational Administration 13 (October):98-106.

REISS, A. and RHODES, A. (1961). "The distribution of juvenile delinquency in the social class structure." American Sociological Review 26 (October):720-732.

SCHAFER, W. and OLEXA, C. (1971). Tracking and opportunity: The locking-out process and beyond. San Francisco: Chandler.

SCHAFER, W., OLEXA, C., and POLK, K. (1970). "Programmed for social class: Tracking in high school." Transaction 7 (October):39-46.

SEEMAN, M. (1959). "On the meaning of alienation." American Sociological Review 24 (December):783-791.

SEXTON, P. (1961). Education and income: Inequalities of opportunity in our public schools. New York: Viking.

STINCHCOMBE, A. (1964). Rebellion in a high school. Chicago: Quadrangle.

THOMAS, C. (1977). The effect of legal sanctions on juvenile delinquency: A comparison of the labeling and deterrence perspectives. Final report submitted to the National Institute of Juvenile Justice and Delinquency Prevention.

THOMAS, C., KREPS, G., and CAGE, R. (1977). "An application of compliance theory to the study of juvenile delinquency." Sociology and Social Research 61 (January):156-175.

VINTER, R. and SARRI, R. (1965). "Malperformance in the public school: A group work approach." Social Work 10 (January):3-13.

WILLOWER, D., EIDELL, T., and HOY, W. (1967). The school and pupil control ideology. University Park: Pennsylvania State University, No. 24.

Rand D. Conger
University of Georgia

FROM SOCIAL LEARNING TO CRIMINAL BEHAVIOR

More than ten years have passed since initial attempts were made to explicate a learning theory of criminal behavior based on principles of operant psychology (Burgess and Akers, 1966; Jeffrey, 1965). Although some critics have faulted these early statements on logical grounds (Adams, 1973; Taylor et al., 1973), little or no basic research has been reported that directly tests the approach (Akers, 1977). What evidence is available for assessing this perspective comes largely from intervention programs or from reanalysis of data intended for other purposes (Adams, 1973; Akers, 1977; Conger, 1976).

From a sociology of knowledge standpoint, an interesting question to ask is why learning theory has suffered such neglect. Certainly, the fact that the propositions involved depend heavily on work done in another discipline has slowed their acceptance by sociologists. But sociologists often borrow from other fields of inquiry, including psychology, and this variable alone does not account for the lack of interest in a learning model of criminality.

Rather, two other factors appear at least equally responsible for this phenomenon. To begin with, the principles of operant psychology are extremely abstract, and their application to specific instances of social behavior is not always straightforward. Therefore, other statements must be used to link these somewhat remote propositions to problems of sociological interest. In addition, at the time learning principles were being introduced as a possible explanation for criminal activities, the emphasis in sociological studies of deviance shifted from etiology to societal reaction. In effect, the questions these learning theories of deviance were designed to answer no longer represented the major focus of sociological inquiry.

This paper will address these latter two issues: the problem of abstractness and the shifts in interest within the sociology of deviance. First, the suggestion will be made that the use of a differential association model, as employed by Burgess and Akers (1966), is only one possible vehicle for incorporating operant principles in a general theory of criminal behavior. Indeed, as Akers (1977) has already noted, several other perspectives are quite consistent with a learning approach. Of special importance in this discussion will be an examination of social control theory (Hirschi, 1969) and how it complements a peer influence model.

The next step in this analysis will move attention from the deviant to other aspects of the social control process. That is, if learning principles are truly general, they should relate not only to the behavior of the condemned individual but also to the activities of those who define and react to unconventional practices. Indeed, social exchange mechanisms are implicit in current attempts to explain how norms develop. It will be suggested that the learning perspective provides as much theoretical grist for the study of lawmakers and enforcers, then, as for the understanding of lawbreakers.

DEVIANT BEHAVIOR

Numerous sociologists, representing diverse theoretical perspectives, have sought to view social interaction as interpersonal exchange (Stryker, 1977). Within this group exists a subset of theorists who draw directly upon the propositions of operant psychology (Burgess and Bushell, 1969; Emerson, 1972; Homans, 1974). Analyses by Emerson, Homans, and others have illustrated how these highly abstract principles relate to diverse areas of social inquiry. While sociologists have most often used exchange theory terminology to apply operant principles to social phenomena, social learning theory, behavior theory, and several other behavioral approaches to the study of social interaction are also based on operant principles. For that reason, while many subtle distinctions may be observed in the process, exchange and learning perspectives are equated in this discussion.

As Emerson (1969) has shown, behavior principles tell us nothing, in and of themselves, about social interaction. This is so because "as propositions become more and more general, they tell us less and less about more and more" (p. 382). Both a problem and a strength of principles like differential reinforcement is the fact that they apply not only to the behavior of people but to the activities of other species as well. Moreover, while they may relate to certain social processes, they also deal with the behaviors of an isolated organism in interaction with its physical environment.

If reinforcement principles are to aid us in explaining social phenomena, then, they must be connected to such events through a series of new statements, each of which contributes certain new information not specifically dealt with by the operant psychologist. For example, situational cues (discriminative stimuli) that identify which behaviors will be reinforced or punished are extremely general in nature; thus, "a group norm has all of the attributes of an S^D (it is an S^D) plus other attributes. All norms are S^Ds, but not all S^Ds are norms" (Emerson, 1969:382). In other words, new terms beyond those of operant psychology must be introduced to a learning theory of social behavior in order to provide substance, or predictive power, within the paradigm.

By building upon the work of Sutherland, Burgess and Akers (1966) created a link between the empirical generalizations of operant research and criminal behaviors. By using intermediate statements from Sutherland's theory, they made operant principles applicable to specific social events. As a result of their reformulation of differential association, Burgess and Akers have been criticized for distorting Sutherland (Taylor et al., 1973), for failing to incorporate processes of punishment and satiation within their propositions (Adams, 1973) and for using a "soft" form of behaviorism (Jeffrey, 1976).

Whatever the shortcomings of the Burgess and Akers approach, however, the important point to emphasize is that their attempt, and others like it, are necessary ventures if operant principles are to provide a starting point for a theory of deviant behavior. The issues they raise remain valid even if the propositions they outline contain some logical imperfections or fail to address specifically some aspects of the operant model. For example, in the study of juvenile delinquency we still do not know, in a systematic way, just what the important reinforcers or punishers are for adolescent populations. We do not know how these contingent stimuli might vary as a function of age, community type, social setting (e.g., family or peer group) or with the passage of time. In sum, empirical work is needed to test and modify the differential association-reinforcement theory to see whether even its most basic ideas can be supported.

Disregarding the gap in research evidence, however, what is clear is that the Burgess and Akers approach is primarily a motivational theory of individual deviance. That is, its primary goal is to illustrate the stimulus control mechanisms that induce and maintain criminality. Even though the same or equivalent reinforcers are suggested to account for normative behavior, the emphasis is clearly on the manner in which social groups and, secondarily, nonsocial circumstances provide the impetus to deviate. In Hirschi's (1969) terms, social learning is a "why do they do it" theory. Indeed, the principal support for its relevance to delinquent conduct is found in the overwhelming evidence from a number of studies that the number of deviant associates one has is the best single predictor of similar conduct by a respondent (Akers, 1977; Conger, 1976; Hirschi, 1969; Meier and Johnson, 1977; Schulz et al., 1977). To date, however, the specific reinforcement that confederates provide for such behavior is almost always inferred rather than demonstrated.

In contrast with the social learning approach, the version of social control theory postulated by Hirschi (1969) addresses the contingencies that promote conformity. "Why don't we all deviate?" rather than "Why do some people deviate?" is the question of interest for Hirschi. Specifically, the social control perspective suggests that people are bonded to society through their attachments, commitments, beliefs, and involvements with their conventional elements. To the extent that this bond is weakened, individuals are free to engage in criminal activities, although no specific motivation to do so is required.

Thus, for a learning perspective, criminality is maintained primarily by social reinforcement. For control theory, the failure to deviate is explained by attachments to conventionality. Of interest here is the fact that these attachments can be understood largely in terms of operant principles. For example, when students do well in school and find their home life rewarding, conventional activities are maintained and these juveniles are not as likely as their less fortunate peers to engage in deviant behavior. Importantly, Wolf (1976) and his associates, who have been intervening with delinquent youth for several years in the Achievement Place group home in Lawrence, Kansas, have begun to identify at a behavioral level some of the reinforcers which help to create this bond of attachment. Youth reports have shown that specific behaviors of group home parents, e.g., manner of speech, are highly valued, and when these events predominate in the home, the probability of delinquent incidents is reduced.

Both the peer influence model and the social bonding perspective, then, can serve as intermediate statements connecting general learning principles to criminal behavior.

Moreover, each theory stresses a different function of reinforcement processes. The first emphasizes the influence of deviant social environments, the second the reinforcement value of conventional social situations. Taken together, an integration of the two perspectives provides a more complete explanation for criminal conduct than either taken alone. And while a formal attempt to do so is beyond the scope of this paper, it is clear that such an integration can likely be accomplished using principles of operant psychology.

At the individual or social psychological level, then, learning principles have obvious utility in attempts to explain deviant behavior. That they do so by using linking statements already found in the sociological literature illustrates the usefulness of Emerson's (1969) analysis on the necessity for finding such links.

The fact that learning notions may play an important role in the etiology of deviance, however, should not be construed to mean that all variance in such behavior is accounted for by them. The extent of the argument being made here is that these principles are important to some as yet unspecified degree. There are certainly unresolved issues within the operant paradigm itself (Stryker, 1977), including questions concerning individual conditionability (Eysenck, 1977) and biological predispositions that differentially influence the behavior of various species (Herrnstein, 1977).

However, even with the controversies that remain, there is no doubt that reinforcement processes do have a tremendous impact on the interaction of people in social settings (McGinnies and Ferster, 1971). Although biological, cognitive or social structural constraints (these constraints can be viewed as reinforcement contingencies) provide given or limiting conditions which affect these principles, the principles themselves appear to apply to a wide range of human activities. Our understanding of social behavior, deviant or conforming, will be incomplete without taking them into account.

Thus far, I have attempted to show the logic involved in moving from these abstract propositions to individual criminality. The next task is to explore their value as mechanisms that help to explain other facets of the social control process, i.e., the production and enforcement of norms. The steps involved will be the same as those used in examining individual deviance.

SOCIAL CONTROL

These next tentative remarks address the question, How might principles of operant psychology be used to explain the seemingly universal proclivity of social groups to make and enforce rules? As already noted, reinforcement processes alone will tell us nothing about social control. Rather, they have utility only when some model involving additional concepts applies them to social phenomena. The linkages necessary to construct a theoretical bridge between reinforcement principles and social control processes will need to: (a) consider the developmental history which characterizes rule-making; (b) apply to groups as well as to individuals; and (c) consider the influence of differential power on social arrangements.

Conflict, Power, and Social Exchange

A major focus of both the labeling and conflict perspectives (the two approaches most often used to explain reactions to deviance) is the differential power held by social groups. Labeling theorists often discuss the power discrepancies which allow social control agents to manipulate client populations. However, the labeling perspective has failed to develop any meaningful theory concerning the social reaction process. Rather, conflict notions are employed in a common sense fashion to account for the differences between labelers and deviants (Akers, 1977). Since a social exchange theory based on operant principles is primarily a theory of social power or control (Emerson,

1969), we will by-pass the labeling approach and look at some features common to the conflict and exchange perspectives.

While conflict theory is normally assumed to be a macro-sociological endeavor, and exchange notions are most often applied to microphenomena, Davis (1975) clearly involves individuals in her explication of the conflict model:

> *Leaders* of large-scale enterprises attempt to extend their own freedom, autonomy, and opportunity for self-interested decision making by repressing the interference, power, and interests of others within their administrative sphere. . . . Large-scale organizations routinize control by making standardized decisions which lump thousands of cases into pre-described categories that are determined by institutional *managers'* hidden agendas. [p. 200]

Consistent with exchange notions, then, Davis is arguing that individuals engage in social control activities in order to maximize their own well-being. In operant terminology, they seek to maximize their own level of reinforcement. However, unlike the pigeon pecking a disc, people usually optimize their own situations through social encounters rather than by manipulating the physical environment alone.

Other features of the conflict perspective also illustrate its compatibility with operantly-based exchange ideas. For example, Davis (1975: 204) states that "authorities . . . negotiate with potential partisans, allocating some resources in *exchange* for compliance." Conformity to norms promulgated by authorities, then, is reinforcing to those in power since they are willing to engage in costly behaviors (e.g., resource allocation) which are valuable to those governed. Patterns of mutual punishment and reward are, by definition, social exchange processes. Moreover, since these patterns of behavior by authorities are instigated, maintained, and at times eliminated by the consequences they produce, they are clearly operant in nature. This statement is true because an operant is any behavior influenced by the events contingent upon it.

However, even though many similarities exist between the exchange and conflict perspectives, certain advantages may be realized by analyzing social control processes using the operant/exchange paradigm. The primary benefit that might accrue by employing an exchange framework, rather than conflict notions alone, is the availability of well-tested empirical generalizations that provide the basis for an operant model of social behavior. These generalizations may suggest a cohesive logical structure for the study of social control mechanisms. For example, while both conflict and exchange theories emphasize the importance of power differentials in the shaping of social arrangements (Davis, 1975; Emerson, 1972), Emerson's (1972) deductions from operant principles have allowed him to describe four possible outcomes that might occur when resources are unequally distributed in a social system.

First, the less powerful partner in a particular situation can increase the value of the resoures s(he) offers in an exchange relationship in order to restore balance to subsequent interactions. For example, those in authority may redistribute wealth in order to maintain the system. Next, one faction can withdraw from the exchange relation or look for other sources for the same valued goods or services. Finally, disadvantaged groups can coalesce to decrease the power of an important source of reinforcement, as labor unions do in their negotiations with management. Interestingly, Davis (1975), without specifying how they are logically derived from conflict ideas, suggests very similar processes in her construction of a conflict approach to deviance.

Other principles from an operant/exchange model could be used to describe and explain similar processes which occur within and between social groups. For example, answers to questions concerning the long-term effects of punishment might gain first insights from work done in the laboratory (Hutchinson, 1977). Indeed, the outcomes of resource disparities described by Emerson are as yet only suggestive and their specific application to various social and historical situations has only just begun (see Dowd, 1975, for an exchange analysis of power changes occurring among the aged).

Clearly, the application of an exchange or learning perspective to explanations of social control will be a complex matter. To illustrate, the support of most people for norms condemning crimes related to personal property and safety (Newman, 1976) probably results from negative reinforcement. That is, most citizens who condone police activities probably do so in an attempt to reduce risks to their own well-being in the loss of material goods or physical harm to their persons. On the other hand, instances of positive reinforcement may also affect the social control processes. For example, members of social control agencies may at times seek to extend their areas of influence in order to increase the security of their positions (Lerman, 1975). That is, the creation of new norms and enforcement policies might rely on positive as well as negative reinforcement. Whatever the particular mechanisms involved, the entire set of operant principles may help to guide and organize theoretical understanding of seemingly diverse social control phenomena.

Macroanalyses

To this point, it has been assumed that the consequences of one's actions affect future behavior whether the unit of analysis is a person or a group. Since groups of people are responsible for norms and reactions to their violation, the proposition that principles which apply at the individual level pertain to group actions as well must be demonstrated.

Fortunately, an increasing amount of empirical evidence suggests that group processes are functionally related to the consequences they produce. Wiggins (1969), for example, showed that the distribution of resources in a group, whether egalitarian or hierarchical, is a direct result of the outcomes associated with each type of structure. When egalitarian practices maximized rewards for the groups

Wiggins studied, it became the structure of choice. The reverse was true when stratification produced the greatest benefit for the group as a whole.

Leik (1972) found that stratification systems can be predicted and controlled when potential exchange resources are known in advance. In Leik's study, cliques, or social strata, were found to form within a small group setting as a direct result of resource compatibility (i.e., those with the greatest resources to exchange interacted together, while those with the least formed separate social units). In another study, Burgess (1969) demonstrated that the structure of communication networks resulted not from spatial relationships between interactants but from the pay-off associated with a given network. Importantly, Pitcher et al., (1978) have demonstrated that the behavioral priniciples which apply to groups in experimental settings are also predictive of group activities in real-world environments.

In sum, operant principles as adapted by social exchange theorists have been shown to apply to the actions of groups as well as to those of individuals. Moreover, these principles, used in a social context, contain the seeds of a theory of social power that addresses the same issues which concerns a conflict perspective of social control. For as Davis (1975:216) notes, power amounts to nothing more than the differential distribution of resources in a social exchange network. In sum, a conflict perspective adds little to exchange notions which are more firmly grounded within a tradition of empirical research. However, the final question we must ask is whether or not exchange principles can deal with historical aspects of the social control process, an important issue for conflict theorists (Davis, 1975).

The Development of
Social Control Mechanisms

Perhaps the most distinguishing feature of operant analysis is its emphasis on the development, maintenance, and termination of behavior (Sidman, 1960). Literally hundreds of hours are spent studying the effects of behavioral consequences on the future course of an individual's, or a group's, activities (Burgess and Bushell, 1969). In addition, Homans (1969) and Kunkel (1966) have shown how the employment of this developmental perspective can be applied to social change occurring at an institutional level. As yet, empirical research has not demonstrated the predictive significance of these admittedly post hoc analyses. However, as we develop better descriptive information concerning what events are or are likely to become reinforcing for specific social groups, the possibility of prediction and explanation within an historical context should approximate that found within experimental settings.

SUMMARY

Two objectives guided the course of this discussion. First, I hoped to illustrate the utility of operant principles in the explanation of individual criminality. While the most commonly cited vehicle for making the transition to deviant behavior from the abstract generalizations of operant research is differential association, other linking statements are possible. Social control theory was suggested as an approach both complementary to social learning theory and also consistent with propositions of operant psychology.

Since behavioral principles are general in nature, it was next suggested that they should apply not only to the actions of deviants but also to those who create and enforce social norms. Discussion showed that an operantly-oriented theory of social exchange is a paradigm concerned basically with social power. While this emphasis on differential resource allocation is consistent with a conflict model of social control, the large number of empirical generalizations upon which exchange notions are based offer certain advantages for theory construction. Finally, it was shown that a learning or exchange perspective contains principles that apply both to groups and historical processes—features necessary to any theory of social control.

The social learning model is based, with some modification, on the principles of operant psychology. Terms like learning theory, social learning, behavior theory, and social exchange have been used interchangeably in this paper because of their common reliance on these principles. But as Emerson (1969) has noted, the generalizations of experimental psychology tell us nothing, by themselves, about social phenomena. Their value for studies of social relationships, as illustrated in the present discussion, is achieved in combination with sociological concepts. The aim of this paper has been to analyze their utility, when combined with less abstract linking statements, in studies of criminal behavior both from the standpoint of individual deviance and of more general social control processes. Hopefully, the tentative steps toward theory which have been outlined here will provide some impetus for more substantial applications of learning principles to the study of rule-making and enforcement, in addition to their current use in etiological research on deviance.

REFERENCES

ADAMS, R. (1973). "Differential association and learning principles revisited." Social Problems 20:447-458.

AKERS, R. L. (1977). Deviant behavior: A social learning approach. Belmont, Calif.: Wadsworth.

BURGESS, R. L. (1969). "Communication networks: An experimental re-evaluation." In R. L. Burgess and D. Bushell (eds.), Behavioral sociology: The experimental analysis of social process. New York: Columbia University Press.

——— and AKERS, R. L. (1966). "A differential association-reinforcement theory of criminal behavior." Social Problems 14:128-147.

——— and BUSHELL, D. (1969). "A behavioral view of some sociological concepts. In R. L. Burgess and D. Bushell (eds.), Behavioral sociology: The experimental analysis of social process. New York: Columbia University Press.

CONGER, R. D. (1976). "Social control and social learning models of delinquent behavior: a synthesis." Criminology 14:17-40.

DAVIS, N. J. (1975). Sociological constructions of deviance: perspectives and issues in the field. Dubuque, Iowa: Wm. C. Brown.

DOWD, J. J. (1975). "Aging as exchange: a preface to theory." Journal of Gerontology 30:584-594.

EMERSON, R. (1969). "Operant psychology and exchange theory." In R. L. Burgess and D. Bushell (eds.), Behavioral sociology: The experimental analysis of social process. New York: Columbia University Press.

EMERSON, R. (1972). "Exchange theory, part I: a psychological basis for social exchange." In J. Berger, M. Zelditch, Jr., and B. Anderson (eds.), Sociological theories in progress. Boston: Houghton Mifflin.

EYSENCK, H. J. (1977). Crime and personality. London: Routledge & Kegan Paul.

HERRNSTEIN, R. J. (1977). "The evolution of behaviorism." American Psychologist 32:593-603.

HIRSCHI, T. (1969). Causes of delinquency. Berkeley: University of California Press.

HOMANS, G. C. (1969). "The sociological relevance of behaviorism." In R. L. Burgess and D. Bushell (eds.), Behavioral sociology: The experimental analysis of social process. New York: Columbia University Press.

——— (1974). Social behavior: Its elementary forms. New York: Harcourt Brace Jovanovich.

HUTCHINSON, R. R. (1977). "By-products of aversive control." In W. K. Honig and J.E.R. Staddon (eds.), Handbook of operant behavior. Englewood Cliffs, N.J.: Prentice-Hall.

JEFFERY, C. R. (1965). "Criminal behavior and learning theory." Journal of Criminal Law, Criminology, and Police Science 56:294-300.

——— (1976). "Theories of deviance: an integrated approach through learning theory." Presented at the annual meeting of the American Society of Criminology, Tucson, Arizona (November).

KUNKEL, J. H. (1966). "Some behavioral aspects of systems analysis." Pacific Sociological Review:12-22.

LEIK, R. K. (1972). "The emergence and change of stratification in social exchange systems." Institute for Sociological Research, University of Washington, Seattle.

LERMAN, P. (1975). Community treatment and social control: A critical analysis of juvenile correctional policy. Chicago: University of Chicago Press.

McGINNIES, E. and FERSTER, C. B. (1971). The reinforcement of social behavior. Boston: Houghton-Mifflin.

MEIER, R. F. and JOHNSON, W. T. (1977). "Deterrence as social control: the legal and extralegal production of conformity." American Sociological Review 42: 292-304.

NEWMAN, G. Comparative deviance. New York: Elsevier.

PITCHER, B. L., HAMBLIN, R. L., and MILLER, J. L. L. (1978). "Diffusion of collective violence." The American Sociological Review 43:23-35.

SCHULZ, B., BOHRNSTEDT, G. W., BORGATTA, E. F., and EVANS, R. R. (1977). "Explaining premarital sexual intercourse among college students: a causal model." Social Forces 56:148-165.

SIDMAN, M. (1960). Tactics of scientific research: Evaluating experimental data in psychology. New York: Basic Books.

STRYKER, S. (1977). "Developments in 'two social psychologies': Toward an appreciation of mutual relevance." Sociometry 40:145-160.

TAYLOR, I., WALTON, P., and YOUNG, J. (1973). The new criminology: For a social theory of deviance. New York: Harper & Row.

WIGGINS, J. A. (1969). "Status differential external consequences, and alternative reward distributions." In R. L. Burgess and D. Bushell (eds.), Behavioral sociology: The experimental analysis of social process. New York: Columbia University Press.

WOLF, M. M. (1976). "Social validity: the case for subjective measurement." Presented at the annual meeting of the American Psychological Association, Washington, D.C. (September).

Paul J. Brantingham
Patricia L. Brantingham
Simon Fraser University

7

A THEORETICAL MODEL OF CRIME SITE SELECTION

Over the years since publication of Jeffery's pioneering article (1969), Crime Prevention Through Environmental Design (CPTED) has developed into a robust sub-area of criminology. Many studies, experiments, and projects have been undertaken. But there is an intellectual distancing between the mainstream of criminology and the environmental design approach.

Many criminologists equate CPTED with simple environmental determinism, a theoretical perspective which places human behavior in a direct cause-and-effect relationship with the physical environment (Reppetto, 1976; Whisenand, 1977:140; Quinney, 1975:249). Such views were very popular, of course, at the beginning of this century: witness the redevelopments of North American slums which were undertaken around 1900 on the simple faith that the improving of physical conditions, in and of itself, would eliminate such social problems as disease and crime (Scott, 1971); and consider statements to such effect by a major criminologist such as Ferri (1896:123).

Environmental determinism, in its simplistic form, is clearly untenable. One of the few things that criminologists have firmly demonstrated is that patterns of human (and perforce, of criminal) behavior are remarkably variable and barely replicable; and single, simple causal models fare poorly in describing what we can observe of crime (Walker, 1974). The ongoing debate between conflict theorists and consensus theorists, fueled by divergent empirical evidence, would not be possible if human behavior were fixed in immutable patterns (Chiricos and Waldo, 1976; see also the ensuing debate on their article—Greenberg, 1977; Hopkins, 1977; Reasons, 1977; Chiricos and Waldo, 1977). Current environmental designers seem to reject determinism and adopt a more probabilistic view of the environment and its impact on behavior (Porteous, 1977:138).

Environmental probabilism asserts that lawful relationships between the environment and behavior exist, but that these relationships are probabilistic rather than certain. At any point in time many paths of action lay open to an individual, and predicting individual behavior absolutely is impossible; but predicting behavior within a degree of uncertainty is possible (Porteous, 1977:138).

Students of CPTED appear to follow this probabilistic approach to environmental design. But while the current perspective accepts environmental probabilism, there has been little in the way of attempts to develop theoretical structures which relate to and help order a growing body of empirically observed regularities between crimes and their environments. Newman, for instance (1972), developed a rationale for target choice by criminals, but this rationale, which used concepts of private, semi-public, and public space, is really just an adaptation of conventional urban design wisdom (Chermayeff and Alexander, 1963) to the problem of crime. His adaptation of these ideas sparked the interest of criminologists, but the rationale seems to create more theoretical problems than it solves and has lately been subjected to severe criticism in both the criminological (Bottoms, 1974) and the urban design (Mawby, 1977) literature.

Jeffery (1977, 1976), a theoretician, goes much further than Newman and develops an abstract framework for thinking about the placement of crimes within the environment. This framework can serve as a starting point for the elaboration of detailed theoretical models. Jeffery argues that the environment is complex, composed simultaneously of physical and social elements, and that people and their environments constantly interact with and impact upon each other (the process of behavior).

Starting from Jeffery's framework, this paper represents an attempt to construct a more detailed theoretical model of criminal behavior within the environment. The paper will consist of three parts: (1) a statement of propositions which forms the basis of the theoretical model; (2) an elaboration of the propositions indicating sources of empirical and conceptual support; and (3) a brief summary.

PROPOSITIONS

I. Individuals exist who are motivated to commit specific offenses.

   (a) The sources of motivation are diverse. Different etiological models or theories appropriately may be invoked to explain the motivation of different individuals or groups.

   (b) The strength of such motivation varies.

   (c) The character of such motivation varies from affective to instrumental.

II. Given the motivation of an individual to commit an offense, the actual commission of an offense is the end result of a multi-staged decision process which seeks out and identifies, within the general environment, a target or victim positioned in time and space.

   (a) In the case of high-affect motivation, the decision process will probably involve a minimal number of stages.

   (b) In the case of high-instrumental motivation, the decision process locating a target or victim may include many stages and much careful searching.

III. The environment emits many signals, or cues, about its physical, spatial, cultural, legal and psychological characteristics.

   (a) These cues can vary from generalized to detailed.

IV. An individual motivated to commit a crime uses cues (either learned through experience or learned through social transmission) from the environment to locate and identify targets or victims.

V. As experiential knowledge grows, an individual motivated to commit an offense learns which individual cues, clusters of cues, and sequences of cues are associated with "good" victims or targets. These cues, cue clusters, and cue sequences (spatial, physical, social, temporal, and so on) can be considered a template which is used in victim or target selection. Potential victims or targets are compared to the template and either rejected or accepted, depending on the congruence.

(a) The process of template construction and the search process may be consciously conducted, or these processes may occur in an unconscious, cybernetic fashion so that the individual cannot articulate how they are done.

VI. Once the template is established, it become relatively fixed and influences future searching behavior, thereby becoming self-reinforcing.

VII. Because of the multiplicity of targets and victims, many potential crime selection templates could be constructed. But because the spatial and temporal distribution of targets and victims is not regular, but clustered or patterned, and because human environmental perception has some universal properties, individual templates have similarities which can be identified.

ELABORATIONS

Proposition I—Motivation for
Criminal Behavior

The first proposition, covering the etiology of criminal motivation, needs no elaboration in this paper. This theoretical model accepts that people are motivated to commit crimes for many different reasons and that many, if not most, of the well-known theories of motivational origin (e.g., learning models, anomie models) are useful in explaining some cases. *This* model assumes motivation and addresses the complementary issue of why particular crimes occur where and when they do. This model attempts to present a reasonable theory of the occurrence of actual criminal events.

Proposition II—Multi-Staged Decision Process in Target Selection

Crime occurrence is not ubiquitous over space and time. From the early 19th-century work of Guerry (1833) and Mayhew (1862) to the classic studies of Shaw and McKay (1969) and Wolfgang (1958) and his students (Amir, 1971; Turner, 1969), and on to contemporary work by Pyle (1974), Baldwin et al. (1976), Capone and Nichols (1976), and our own work (Brantingham and Brantingham, 1975a, 1975b, 1977; Brantingham et al., 1977), it has been shown that crime patterns are not random, but can be described by more specific distributional functions. More interestingly, spatial and temporal patterns can be identified at many levels of environmental aggregation, from the level of individual rooms within buildings to the city-wide level and beyond.

The existence of patterns at many levels of aggregation can be explained in different ways. They might be a function of the categorization process necessary to official recording of data. They might be a product of biologic imperative (e.g., territorial patterning of behavior) or of simple physical determinism of the sort asserted by turn-of-the-century urban planners and criminologists. They might be produced by the far more complex interaction of physical and social patterns described by researchers such as Chapin (1974). We suggest that an explanation of great power is that these observed patterns are the empirical trace of a multi-level decision process.

Etzioni (1968:282-292) describes a decision-making process which he calls mixed-scanning. This process employs hierarchical, sequential decisions which move from broad scanning of all possibilities to detailed investigation of a limited number of possibilities. The hierarchy may have many tiers, depending on the complexity of the task. As examples of this type of decision-making, Etzioni suggests a soldier scanning a field, looking for enemy activity; a weather satellite with two cameras, one for a broad overview trying to locate general categories of cloud formation and the other for detailed analysis of potentially troublesome cloud formations identified by the first camera; and a chess player exploring future moves within general strategies.

We think that the consistently observed regularities in criminal event patterns can be explained, in part, by the idea that an offender follows a multi-staged decision process similar to mixed-scanning in identifying targets or victims. For example, a house burglar may first locate a general area of the city where he feels potential targets exist, say older multi-family housing areas (Reppetto, 1974; Brantingham and Brantingham, 1977, 1975a; Pyle, 1974); then within that general area he may locate sub-areas which offer more anonymity (Brantingham and Brantingham, 1975b; Newman, 1972; Reppetto, 1974), or exhibit generally useful characteristics such as poor street lighting or lots of bushes (Phelan, 1977), or provide easy entry and exit by street (Bevis and Nutter, 1977; Molumby, 1976). Finally, once within the sub-area, a specific housing unit or target will be selected. In areas with a high degree of architectural homogeneity, the detailed target choice may be random, or keyed to specifics such as locks and dogs (Molumby, 1976; Scarr, 1973). In areas with architectural variety, Newmanesque cues may be used. This process is outlined in Letkemann's (1973:137-157) chapter on "casing" by burglars and robbers. Mixed-scanning in police decision processes is described in passing in Sacks (1972). Conklin (1972:87-101) also described this process in regard to robbery.

Several points should be emphasized. First, such a search procedure need not be entirely conscious. Human behavior is not always consciously undertaken. Second, for certain offenses, particularly ones with a high affective level, the actual search process may be minimal. The classic murder, an emotional explosion which takes place within a family or acquaintanceship setting (Wolfgang, 1958) is such a high affect crime. Here, once the motive is created, the search may require no more than looking across the room.

**Proposition III—Cue-Emitting
Potential of the Environment**

When a person interacts with reality, he interacts through his senses. Seeing, hearing, smelling, and touching are tools used to learn about reality. The information man receives through his senses is varied and plentiful. This vast amount of information taken in through the senses is organized, structured, and imbued with meaning by information processing systems which are in part a product of physiological predisposition and in part learned. For example, people learn to judge distance, the friendliness of a dog, or the heat of a stove burner. People learn the complex social spacing mechanisms of the culture in which they live (Hall, 1966; Ashcraft and Scheflen, 1976); and people learn norms of behavior.

The environment emits much information or many stimuli. Not all the information is used by people to form their perceptions.[1] Some information is "used" while most is "ignored." The used information can be considered as "cues."

The "environment" for CPTED and for environmental designers in general is no longer the simple physical reality of turn-of-the-century determinists. It is, instead, considered a more complex reality made up of physical objects, spatial relations, social relations, and a sociocultural backcloth (Golledge et al., 1976; Ittleson et al., 1974; Porteous, 1977).

The environment can also be perceived at many levels. For example, when driving through an urban area, a person may be aware of residential buildings, commercial buildings, open spaces, major streets, and major structures. The traveler is probably not aware of very detailed characteristics such as small store signs or specific plantings around residential buildings. A person walking along a street, however, may be aware of pavement texture, store displays, plantings, building architectural features. What is perceived depends on the characteristics of the urban environment

(Lynch, 1960; Appleyard, 1969) and the characteristics of the perceiver (Orleans, 1973; Porteous, 1977). Patterns of perception, however, are evident.

Proposition IV—Crime Cues

The environment emits "cues" (or, people interpret information from the environment as "cues") which people use to help them function and move about. Specifically, the environment emits "cues" which are used by criminals to locate victims or targets in time and space. Indirect evidence of such cues can be seen in the numerous studies which correlate crime occurrence data with physical and nonphysical aspects of crime sites (Pyle, 1974; Brantingham and Brantingham, 1975b, 1977; Newman, 1972; Jeffery, 1976). Hints of more direct evidence can be found in a number of studies which explore how criminals select targets (Reppetto, 1974; Letkemann, 1973; Phelan, 1977) or examine the environmental perceptions of "criminals" and "noncriminals" with respect to the same urban settings (McConnell, 1976).

The existence of environmental factors which are associated with patterns of crime occurrence can be tied together with the multi-level decision process. The decision process can be conceived of as using the cues from the environment to help select the path toward a victim or target. Other elements, of course, are part of the decision process. The motivation of an individual, his psychological background, his sociological background, and his past history of criminal behavior influence the multi-staged decision-making as well as the situational aspects in the environment.[2]

**Proposition V—Cue Learning
Leading to Template Construction**

Individual cues can be associated with "good" targets or victims. For example, the presence of a convenience store may be associated with "good robbery target" (Capone and Nichols, 1976; Duffala, 1976). Clusters of cues may also be associated with targets. For example, a "good robbery target" in Tallahassee, Florida, has lately exhibited the following cue cluster: a convenience store, late at night, near a major highway, but also by open land (Duffala, 1976). A sequence of cues or a sequence of cue clusters may become associated with "good targets." For example, a convenience store off the main road may become associated with a "good target" if it is found after a period of "casing" or if it exhibits additional cues (e.g., cash register at side of store, windows obscured by signs) after entry to make a purchase.

Cues, cue clusters, and cue sequences, of course, need not derive exclusively from the physical components of the environment. Social situations such as arguments before an assault (Curtis, 1974), illicit sexual relations before a robbery (Conklin, 1972:92), or a group gathering of teenagers before a theft (Hindelang, 1976) form environmental cues about the appropriateness of a specific setting for crime. The cues, cue clusters, and cue sequences associated with a specific offense can be considered a "template."

In interpreting the environment, people tend to categorize and generalize. They take a new situation and place it into categories of situations known from previous experience. (Ittleson et al., 1974). Thus, people can recognize a city; it has tall buildings, dense development, and heavy traffic relative to surrounding areas. People recognize specific situations and associated appropriate behaviors (Barker, 1968) such as how to act in a classroom, in a hospital, or in a football stadium. People recognize neighborhoods (Lee, 1968). Since people in general are good at classifying and recognizing, it seems reasonable to assume that criminals learn to recognize potential crime sites or situations. It is also reasonable to assume that criminals can recognize potentially poor crime sites or situations and refrain from criminal behavior in such settings. (Consistent failure to do so may lead to diagnoses of mental illness or psychopathy.) The inappropriateness of criminal behavior in most environments (or "behavior settings," as Barker would call them) may explain the difficult criminological problem of why even the most committed hard-core criminal deviants behave very much like noncriminals, engaging in nondeviant, legal, inoffensive behavior most of the time.

Proposition VI—Relative Endurance
of Crime "Template"

Once a crime template develops, it tends to endure. The endurance of a template can be justified by employing a reinforcing schema. By interacting with the environment and/or through social transmission, a template of a "good" target, victim, setting is constructed. Where this template is used to guide future criminal activities and those activities succeed, then the template is reinforced.

It should be noted, once again, that the process being described need not, and most likely will not, be conscious. The matching of a particular crime site or situation probably consists of locating a place where the would-be criminal feels comfortable, where he feels that his actions will not be interrupted in any serious fashion.

Proposition VII—Limited
Number of Templates

Templates are individual constructions. When descriptions are carried to extreme, we would have to say that each criminal's template with respect to each criminal behavior set is unique. However, there is strong evidence that the variation between templates constructed by different people is not unlimited. Perceptual patterns do emerge, both at the physiological level and the conceptual level.[3] The existence of patterns can be seen best in the work of people who study "mental maps" (Lynch, 1960; Golledge et al., 1976; De Jonge, 1962; Orleans, 1973; Downs and Stea, 1973). All have uncovered patterns in how people perceive space and cities.

Patterns vary by broad socio-demographic characteristics. Knowledge and images of cities increase with age (Porteous, 1977); are generally greater for workers outside the home (Ittleson et al., 1974:293); vary by social class (Orleans, 1973), generally covering a smaller area for the less mobile lower socioeconomic group; and vary by length of residence (Golledge et al., 1969). Other investigators have examined how actual space is deformed or changed through perception and experiences. For example, distances along major travel arteries are perceived as shorter by people who use those arteries than equal distances not on major transportation paths. This shortening of distance is a common experience. Traveling to a "strange" or "new" location usually seems longer than traveling back. Even though studies in environmental perceptions are still in their infancy, patterns do exist.

SUMMARY

Criminals do not move randomly through their environment. Target and site selection procedures produce clear spatial patterning. This paper has proposed an information processing model which can be used to understand the process followed by criminals in searching out and choosing targets. Briefly, the model presupposes that motivation to commit crimes exists, and, if an individual is motivated to commit a crime, the actual commission of the crime depends upon the meeting in time and space of a likely target or victim with a motivated individual. Motivated criminals, through experience or social transmission, create perceptual (or cognitive) generalizations of "likely targets or victims." Motivated individuals, through spatial search processes, try to find targets or victims that match their perceptual generalizations or templates. When a match occurs, a crime is highly probable.

The theoretical model which has been proposed can be used to explore both high-affect and low-affect crimes. However, the importance of different parts of the model varies with the type of crime and the affective level associated with the crime. With low-affect crimes such as burglary or embezzlement, the creation of a crime site template and the matching of opportunity with template is very important. Traditional target hardening projects try to make the matching of opportunity with template difficult. Newmanesque redesign projects also represent attempts to reduce the actual number of locations which match hypothesized crime site templates. In high-affect crimes such as murder, motivation appears to play a larger role and matching of victim with template is more automatic. But even in murder, environment does play a role. The existence of typical murder patterns, such as the husband/wife murder in a dwelling unit, or the acquaintanceship murder near or in a bar, show the strength of environmental triggers in a high-affect crime. Motivation and environment act together.

CPTED, while clearly having an applied side, can also be explored from a theoretical point of view. Criminal behavior involves motivation and action. Environmental design explores the variety of actions which occur and the complex interaction between individuals with biologic and learned characteristics, and the environment.

NOTES

1. Perception is used in a general or common way to refer to the structure or meaning placed on actual complex receptive stimuli. This is the usage adopted by geographers in their studies of environmental perception.

2. It is at the point of conceptual merger of decision-making with cue-emitting characteristics of the environment that environmental probabilism emerges. Direct causal links between immediate crime occurrence environment and crime are not possible. The relationship between environment and crime is mediated by individual motivation, psychological conditions, and sociological conditions, and must be viewed with a softer edge.

3. As was noted above, in accordance with the usual terminology in environmental perception studies, the word "perception" is being used to cover both classical perception and cognition.

REFERENCES

AMIR, M. (1971). Patterns of forcible rape. Chicago: University of Chicago Press.

APPLEYARD, D. (1969). "Why buildings are known." Environment and Behavior 1:131-156.

ASHCRAFT, N. and SCHEFLEN, A.E. (1976). People space: The making and breaking of human boundaries. Garden City, N.Y.: Anchor.

BALDWIN, J., BOTTOMS, A.E., and WALKER, M.A. (1976). The urban criminal: A study in Sheffield. London: Tavistock.

BARKER, R.R. (1968). Ecological psychology. Stanford, Calif.: Stanford University Press.

BEVIS, C. and NUTTER, J.B. (1977). "Changing street layouts to reduce residential burglary." Paper read at the annual meeting of the American Society of Criminology, Atlanta, Georgia.

BOTTOMS, A. E. (1974). "Review of Defensible Space by Oscar Newman." British Journal of Criminology 14:203-206.

BRANTINGHAM, P. and BRANTINGHAM, P. (1975a). "The spatial patterning of burglary." Howard Journal of Penology and Crime Prevention 14:11-24.

―――(1975b). "Residential burglary and urban form." Urban Studies 12:273-284.

―――(1977). "Housing patterns and burglary in a medium-sized American city." In J. E. Scott and S. Dinitz (eds.), Criminal justice planning. New York: Praeger.

――― and MOLUMBY, T. (1977). "Perceptions of crime in a dreadful enclosure." Ohio Journal of Science 77:256-261.

CAPONE, D.L. and NICHOLS, W.W., Jr. (1976). "Urban structure and criminal mobility." American Behavioral Scientist 20:199-213.

CHAPIN, F. S., Jr. (1974). Human activity patterns in the city: Things people do in time and space. New York: John Wiley.

CHERMAYEFF, S. and ALEXANDER, C. (1963). Community and privacy: Toward a new architecture and humanism. Garden City, N.Y.: Doubleday.

CHIRICOS, T.G. and WALDO, G. (1976). "Socioeconomic status and sentencing: An empirical assessment of a conflict proposition." American Sociological Review 40:753-772.

―――(1977). "Reply to Greenberg, Hopkins and Reasons." American Sociological Review 42:181-185.

CONKLIN, J.E. (1972). Robbery and the criminal justice system. Philadelphia: J.P. Lippincott.

CURTIS, L.A. (1974). Criminal violence: National patterns and behavior. Lexington, Mass.: Lexington Books.

DE JONGE, D. (1962). "Images of urban areas: Their structure of psychological foundations." Journal of the American Institute of Planners 28:266-276.

DOWNS, R.M. and STEA, D. (1973). Image & environment: Cognitive mapping and spatial behavior. London: Edward Arnold.

DUFFALA, D.C. (1976). "Convenience stores, armed robbery, and physical environmental features." American Behavioral Scientist 20:227-246.

ETZIONI, A. (1968). The active society. New York: Free Press.

FERRI, E. (1896). Criminal sociology. New York: Appleton-Century-Crofts.

GOLLEDGE, R., BRIGGS, R., and DEMKO, D. (1969). "The configuration of distances in intraurban space." Proceedings of the Association of American Geographers 1:60-65.

GOLLEDGE, R., RiVIZZIGNO, V. L., and SPECTOR, A. (1976). "Learning about a city: Analysis by multi-dimensional scaling." Pp. 95-116 in R. Golledge (ed.), Spatial choice and spatial behavior. Columbus: Ohio State University Press.

GREENBERG, D.F. (1977). "Socioeconomic status and criminal sentences: Is there an association?" American Sociological Review 42:174-176.

GUERRY, A.M.(1833) Essai sur la Statistique Moral de la France. Paris: Chez Crochard.

HALL, E.T. (1966). The hidden dimension. Garden City, N.Y.: Doubleday.

HINDELANG, M.J. (1976). "With a little help from their friends: Group participation in reported delinquent behavior." British Journal of Criminology 16:109-125.

HOPKINS, A. (1977). "Is there a class bias in criminal sentencing?" American Sociological Review 42:176-177.

ITTLESON, W.H., PROSHANSKY, H.M., RIVLIN, L.G., and WINKEL, G.H. (1974). An introduction to environmental psychology. New York: Holt, Rinehart & Winston.

JEFFERY, C.R. (1969). "Crime prevention and control through environmental engineering." Criminologica 7:35-58.
————— (1976). "Criminal behavior and the physical environment." American Behavioral Scientist 20:149-174.
————— (1977). Crime prevention through environmental design. Beverly Hills, Calif.: Sage.
LEE, T. R. (1968). "Urban neighborhood as a socio-spatial schema." Human Relations 21:241-267.
LETKEMANN, P. (1973). Crime as work. Englewood Cliffs, N.J.: Prentice-Hall.
LYNCH, K. (1960). The image of the city. Cambridge, Mass.: MIT Press.
MAWBY, R. I. (1977). "Defensible space: A theoretical and empirical appraisal." Urban Studies 14:169-179.
MAYHEW, H. (1862). London labour and the London poor, vol. IV. London: Charles Griffin.
McCONNELL, M. V. (1976). "Criminal v. non-criminal differential edge perception." Department of Urban and Regional Planning, Florida State University. (unpublished)
MOLUMBY, T. (1976). "Patterns of crime in a university housing project." Amercan Behavioral Scientist 20:247-259.
NEWMAN, O. (1972). Defensible space: Crime prevention through urban design. New York: Macmillan.
ORLEANS, P. (1973). "Differential cognition of urban residents: Effects of social scale on mapping." Pp. 115-130 in R. Downs and D. Stea (eds.), Image & Environment. London: Edward Arnold.
PHELAN, G.F. (1977). "Testing 'academic' notions of architectural design for burglary prevention: How burglars perceive cues of vulnerability in suburban apartment complexes." Paper read at the annual meeting of the American Society of Criminology, Atlanta, Georgia.
PORTEOUS, J. D. (1977). Environment & behavior: Planning and everyday urban life. Reading, Mass.: Addison-Wesley.
PYLE, G.F. (1974). "The spatial dynamics of crime." University of Chicago, Department of Geography, Research Paper #159.
QUINNEY, R. (1975). Criminology. Boston: Little, Brown.
REASONS, C.E. (1977). "On methodology, theory and ideology." American Sociological Review 42:177-181.
REPPETTO, T.A. (1974). Residential crime. Cambridge, Mass.: Ballinger.
————— (1976) "Crime prevention through environmental policy: A critique." American Behavioral Scientist 20:275-288.
SACKS, H. (1972) "Notes on police assessment of moral character." Pp. 280-293 in D. Sudnow (ed.), Studies in social interaction. New York: Free Press.
SCARR, H. (1973). Patterns of burglary. Washington, D.C.: U. S. Department of Justice, NILECJ of the LEAA.
SCOTT, M. (1971). American city planning since 1890. Berkeley: University of California Press.
SHAW, C.R. and McKAY, H. D. (1969). Juvenile delinquency and urban areas. Chicago: University of Chicago Press.
TURNER, S. (1969). "Delinquency and distance." Pp. 11-26 in T. Sellin and M. E. Wolfgang (eds.), Delinquency: Selected studies. New York: John Wiley.
WALKER, N. (1974). "Lost causes in criminology." Pp. 47-62 in R. Hood (ed.), Crime, criminology, and public policy. London: Heinemann.
WHISENAND, P. M. (1977). Crime prevention. Boston: Holbrook Press.
WOLFGANG, M.E. (1958). Patterns in criminal homicide. Philadelphia: University of Pennsylvania Press.

Gary F. Jensen
Maynard L. Erickson
University of Arizona

8

THE SOCIAL MEANING
OF SANCTIONS

In their introduction to *Perception in Criminology,* Richard
Henshel and Robert Silverman (1975) note that a perceptual
orientation has been growing in the field of criminology
which parallels and draws on lines of inquiry in general
sociology such as ethnomethodology, Schutzian phenomenology, symbolic interactionism, and the sociology of
knowledge. In fact, this orientation is reflected in the study
of a wide range of criminological topics. For example, one
area where a blend of quantitative analysis and a concern
with subjective states is especially prominent at present
is in the study of deterrence. In the last few years numerous
articles have appeared in print (Bailey and Lott, 1967;
Kraut, 1976; Silberman, 1965; Teevan, 1965; Grasmick
and Milligan, 1976) relating "beliefs" about the certainty
of punishment to criminal or delinquent activity. Theoretical
discourse on deterrence has come to stress the view that "a
system of deterrence is a system of communication that
attempts to convey the message that, for persons who have
committed a criminal act, 'justice' is certain and terrible"
(Geerken and Gove, 1975:497).

Another area where this trend is likely to develop is in
the study of labeling and specific deterrence. While often
presented as polar opposites, several theorists (Thorsell

AUTHORS' NOTE: This research was supported by a research grant from the
National Institute of Mental Health (MH22350).

and Klemke, 1972; Tittle, 1975) have suggested that the effects of labeling or sanctioning may vary by social setting. Thus, while the focus of most research has been on the behavior of the labeled (Mahoney, 1974), a few studies can be found operating from a theoretical base which emphasizes the variable "meaning" or "personal relevance" of labeling in different subgroups (Jensen, 1972; Ageton and Elliott, 1974; Harris, 1976). Such an approach is similar to that reflected in the statements above about deterrence theory. The study of labeling and sanctioning should not be limited to the objective properties of reactions to deviance, but should consider the actor's subjective images of the nature, probability, and consequences of such reactions. Moreover, the emphasis on meaning and subjective states does not have to entail an atomistic focus on individuals. Rather, it is assumed that such states are a social as well as an individual construction; that there is order or structure to the social meaning of sanctions.

This paper explores several questions relevant to the study of perceptual or subjective aspects of sanctions. First, what types of effects, costs, or consequences of sanctioning concern people the most, and is there order or structure to such concerns? Concerning the first question, pain and suffering associated with physical punishment and the deprivation of biological and social needs would seemingly be accepted by most people as potential costs of apprehension for law-breaking. The dominant focus in deterrence research has been on the costs of law-breaking defined in terms of such legal consequences (Gibbs, 1968; Tittle, 1969; Gray and Martin, 1969; Logan, 1972; Ehrlich, 1972; Bailey and Smith, 1972; Erickson and Gibbs, 1973). However, a much broader conception of costs is implicated in sociological notions such as "stigmatization" (the imputation of a socially devalued image to the law-breaker) where the emphasis is on the consequences of labeling in the actor's social environment and the subsequent consequences for the actor's self-image. In fact, publicity campaigns aimed at reducing crime such as shoplifting emphasize the stigma associated with acquiring a "record" rather than the actual punishment delivered by the formal sanctioning system. Moreover, some major brands of criminological theory focus on the perceived costs of apprehension in terms of investments, commitments, or "stakes" in the system as *the* major barriers to law-breaking (Hirschi, 1969; Nye, 1958; Briar and Piliavin, 1965). The emphasis is on the deterrent impact of perceived ramifications in the actor's social environment.

In this investigation we consider three distinct types of consequences or potential costs of labeling for an actor: (1) formal punishments; (2) the reactions of significant others; and (3) restricted opportunities to realize common success goals. In this case, formal punishment refers to possible sanctions meted out by official agents of control after apprehension. Such sanctions are central to the notion of legal or "formal" deterrence. The latter two categories of costs are central to delineations of "informal deterrence" and stigmatization. As Geerken and Gove (1975:499) note, "Informal deterrence systems operate largely through interpersonal communication and typically involve sanctions at the interpersonal level." Such informal processes can occur in both primary and secondary relationships, but all tend to center around the "loss of face" or a "good reputation" and the impact of such status loss on an actor's ability to obtain valued ends. Thus, we include the perceived loss of status in the eyes of significant others as well as the consequences for realizing certain goals (getting a good job, going to college, and the like) as informal sanctions.

Another issue to be examined here is whether the perceived costs or ramifications of sanctioning vary systematically among communities, or sociodemographic or other socially differentiated categories. One of the most widely accepted (yet seemingly trivial) observations made by criminologists is the notion that criminal or delinquent behavior is more probable when costs are low (or when rewards outweigh the costs) than when they are high. Such notions have been expressed in one form or another by theorists approaching crime from a number of different directions (Burgess and Akers, 1966; Akers, 1973; Piliavin et al., 1969; Briar and Piliavin, 1965; Hirschi, 1969; Ehrlich,

1972; Tullock, 1974). The major limitation of such claims, however, is that they merely describe a necessary condition in the learning process which must occur for the behavior to occur. Such observations tell us little about the *circumstances* under which these conditions are likely to exist.

There are numerous precedents for positing that the costs of labeling are, in fact, socially structured (i.e., variable among groups, classes, and communities). This assumption is implicit in virtually all sociological theories of crime and delinquency. Whether a product of subcultural values (Sutherland and Cressey, 1974; Miller, 1958), limited legitimate opportunity (Merton, 1957; Cohen, 1955; Cloward and Ohlin, 1960) or variable stakes in the system (Toby, 1957; Briar and Piliavin, 1965; Hirschi, 1969), the potential costs of law-breaking have been depicted as *greater* under some circumstances than others. Generally, the physical and social rewards of crime have been viewed as out-weighing the costs of crime for every group or category with a high crime rate. Thus, we find Geerken and Gove (1975:508-509) positing that "the costs of criminal activity are likely to be greater for those who are well rewarded by the society" and that certain minority groups may have less commitment to the values reflected in the law, diminishing the informal costs of sanctioning. They hypothesized that "the effectiveness of the deterrence system will increase as investments in and rewards for the social system increase." Their arguments would have us predict that the higher an actor's social standing, the greater the perceived social ramifications of labeling.

On the other hand, it has not been convincingly demonstrated that normative stances concerning crime vary significantly by social class or minority status (Hirschi, 1969; Ball-Rokeach, 1973; Rossi et al., 1974). Moreover, opportunities for the most lucrative infractions of the law (white collar crime, many forms of fraud, business crime, graft, corruption, and the like) are limited to those in positions where rewards of the system are great. We can argue that as investments in the system increase the effectiveness of the deterrence system *does not* vary, because the potential benefits of crime increase as well. Costs and rewards may balance each other in that those who have the least to lose are likely to gain the least as well. Obviously, there is considerable room for theoretical debate on the issue.

Other variations which have been addressed by virtually every sociological theory of crime include the predominance of officially recorded crime in metropolitan as compared to rural settings and among males as compared to females. Again, the "costs" of crime in terms of the ramifications of labeling are generally conceived of as greater in rural or small-town settings than metropolitan settings, and greater for females than males. Informal control processes are commonly depicted as much stronger in small than large communities and the very emergence of formal control mechanisms is often attributed to the urban "breakdown" in traditional means of social control by family, group, and community. Thus, we might hypothesize that informal sanctions will be of lesser concern to metropolitan residents than small-town Americans, and that (relative to informal ramifications) the formal ramifications will predominate in urban settings. Regarding gender, we can posit that the perceived costs of labeling will tend to be greater for females than males, particularly with regard to informal ramifications.

The third and final issue to be considered is the relation of various perceived costs of sanctioning to criminality. There have been several studies suggesting that the perceived *risk* of sanctioning is negatively related to self-reported criminality (Jensen, 1969; Silberman, 1976). In fact, in an earlier analysis of the current body of data we report a persistent, nonspurious relationship between measures of perceived personal risk and self-reported delinquency (Jensen et al., 1978). Our concern here, however, is with the nature, distribution, and consequences of the perceived *costs* of sanctioning. When dealing with legal sanctions the analogous difference is between the *certainty* and *severity* of punishment. We are concerned with the perceived severity or costs of labeling in the actor's social environment as distinct from perceived risk of apprehension. If formal deterrence processes are occurring, we should find variations in perceived formal ramifications to be negatively related to involvement in crime. Similarly, we should find perceived informal ramifications to be negatively related to involvement in crime. Moreover, if common sociological arguments about the importance of informal controls are correct, we should find perceived ramifications in an actor's social environment to be more relevant to behavior than formal ramifications.

STUDY DESIGN

The issues outlined above will be examined using survey data collected by means of an anonymous questionnaire administered to 1,700 high school students in 1973-1974 and readministered to over 3,000 students at the same high schools in 1974-1975. Thus, we do not focus on all forms of crime nor on all segments of American society. Rather, we will focus on a particular age group which contributes heavily to many forms of crime in the United States.

The studets encompassed by the survey in 1974-1975 include nearly the total available high school population in two of three small-town communities studied ("Farm Town" and "Mining Town"), and 50% of three urban high schools ("Western," "Central," and "Parochial") representing nearly all students in required English and/or social studies courses, and around 50% of the student body in the one small-town high school which required, for participation in the survey, signed parental consent ("Tourist Town"). Thus, for only one subsample (100 of 3,145 cases) was there a real possibility of self (or parental) selection into the sample during 1974-1975. All other schools allowed either a systematic selection of classrooms to cover all grades or allowed the survey to be given to all students. Parents could withhold permission and students could refuse to participate, but such refusals were rare (less than 5%). The same data were collected in 1973-1974, the first year of the study, which led to a much smaller (N = 1,700) and more questionable sample. However, we have carried out much of the analysis for each school year and, thus, have built in our own replication.

The communities included in this study are all located in southern Arizona. The urban setting is Tucson, with a population of around 400,000. Tucson ranked seventh in terms of crime rates for standard metropolitan statistical areas as reported by the Federal Bureau of Investigation for 1974. It is also one of the fastest-growing cities in the United States according to census data. The three smaller communities range in population from 1,200 to 8,000. One has an economy oriented around ranching, one around mining, and the third is heavily dependent on tourism.

The survey collected data on a wide range of variables relevant to sanctions, but this analysis will concentrate on the perceived costs of labeling. Students were given the hypothetical statement "Suppose you were caught and taken to juvenile court" and then were asked how much each of the following would worry them (to which response categories were "definitely yes," "probably yes," "uncertain," "probably not," and "definitely not"): (1) the police might hurt you; (2) the judge might send you to a reformatory; (3) the judge might put you on probation; (4) how your parents might react; (5) a delinquent record might keep you out of college; (6) a record might keep you from getting a good job; (7) other teenagers might think badly of you; (8) your teachers might think badly of you; (9) you might think badly of yourself.

Students were also presented questions dealing with 18 different delinquent activities and asked to indicate how many times in the last 12 months they had committed each act. The questionnaire was administered anonymously, and students were told that the project was interested in finding how people who had different experiences with the law felt about several issues involving the law. Steps were taken to maximize privacy and anonymity and to assure students that they were not being tricked. The self-report data are used to create an index similar to indices reported in several recent studies of delinquency combining reports of major and minor theft, vandalism, auto theft, assault, and fighting (Hirschi, 1969; Hindelang, 1973; Burkett and White, 1974).

Information on background characteristics was also gathered in the questionnaire. *Gender* is based on student self-classification into male or female, and *ethnic status* is based on self-classification into White (or Anglo), Chicano (or Mexican-American), Indian, Black, Oriental, or "Other." Since the major ethnic categories in the area are Anglo and Chicano, our analysis will be limited to three categories: Anglo, Chicano, and all other minority groups considered together. *Social status* was assessed in terms of father's and mother's educational attainment.

FINDINGS

Perceived Costs

In Table 1 we report the percentage of students answering "yes" or "definitely yes" to each of the perceived cost items outlined above. It appears that the most common concerns among high school students involve the informal ramifications of legal processing. Nearly all indicate that they would worry about parental reactions. Between 79% and 85% would worry about the consequences of legal processing for getting a good job, and between 58% and 75% would worry about a record keeping them out of college. For the sample as a whole, the next most common concern was that the adolescent might think poorly of him/ herself. Around 50% would worry about being put on probation or being sent to a reformatory. These concerns were followed, in order, by teacher reaction, peer reaction, and the possibility of being hurt by the police. Thus, the informal consequences of labeling are foremost in students' minds.

We also found that the order of student concerns is a relatively stable phenomenon from school to school and year to year. Considering all possible pairs of schools, the rank order correlations range from .946 to .996 in 1973-1974 and from .871 to 1.00 in 1974-1975. For the same schools during the two different school years the coefficients ranged from .929 to .996. All coefficients were statistically significant at well beyond the .01 level. In sum, there is definitely a structure to student concerns about sanctions.

Table 1: Perceived Costs of Labeling by School by Year (proportion answering "Yes" and "Definitely Yes") (in percentages)

SETTING:	Small Town						Urban					
SCHOOL:	Mining		Tourist		Farm		Western		Central		Parochial	
YEAR:	1974	1975	1974	1975	1974	1975	1974	1975	1974	1975	1974	1975
Hurt	6	8	2	12	10	10	9	8	9	10	10	13
Kids	25	28	31	44	45	38	33	36	29	32	30	34
Teachers	44	39	44	58	54	44	41	42	40	39	47	48
Reformatory	50	51	51	67	52	57	49	42	47	51	52	54
Self	52	58	63	67	66	61	63	65	65	64	60	59
Probation	54	48	49	53	54	53	49	48	48	46	56	54
College	64	61	72	61	73	60	58	65	59	70	63	75
Job	83	82	85	84	80	82	82	82	79	82	84	87
Parents	90	88	86	92	91	88	90	90	88	90	96	94
(N=)	(290)	(752)	(57)	(106)	(80)	(348)	(483)	(729)	(341)	(766)	(449)	(444)

127

Perceived Costs by
Background Characteristics

We have already observed that the rank ordering of perceived costs is quite stable over time and among communities. However, while the order of perceived costs appears to be constant from setting to setting, we also considered the possibility that the proportions concerned about various ramifications might vary from community to community and among different sociodemographic categories. Combining the three urban schools together, we found only four communal differences which were significant at beyond the .05 level (using chi-square): (1) Farm Town and Tucson youths appear somewhat more concerned with the possibilities of police hurting them than the Tourist Town or Mining Town youths; (2) Tourist Town and Farm Town youths were more concerned about being sent to a reformatory than Tucson and Mining Town youths; (3) Tucson youths were more concerned about a record keeping them out of college than Mining, Tourist, or Farm Town students; and, (4) Tourist Town and Farm Town youths were somewhat more concerned about the impact of labeling for their reputations with other teenagers. In all cases, differences were slight.

In sum, there was no consistent pattern of differences between the metropolitan and small town samples. For three of the four significant associations, the Mining Town youths were lowest in perceived costs. Farm Town and Tourist Town youths tended to be the most concerned in those instances with the exception of the consequences of labeling for college entrance where the urban youths were most concerned. The fact that more of the urban youths plan on going to college would seem to explain why such consequences are more prominent.

Given common images of "big city" versus "small town" life, the similarity in the structure and meaning of sanctions between settings may come as a surprise to many people. However, two studies of delinquency in rural settings have concluded that there are few significant differences between rural or small-town youth and metropolitan youth in official or self-reported delinquency (Clark and Wenninger, 1962; Polk, 1974). Similarly, recent research on rural-urban differences in behavior and attitudes among adults has shown the rural urban variable to make little or no difference (Van Es and Brown, 1974). In this study there was a tendency for Farm Town youths to report the least involvement in delinquency, with Mining Town students reporting the most. Students at the Tucson schools and in the Tourist Town high school tended to fall in between. However, even when significant differences were found, the differences were slight.

We also examined differences in perceived costs by parents' educational status, grade in school, minority status, and gender. Father's educational status was significantly and positively related to five perceived costs: reformatory, college, career, reputation with other teenagers, and self-respect. Mother's educational status was significantly related only to concern over getting into college. While significant, the relationships are all quite weak with gamma coefficients ranging between +.01 and +.16. The most impressive differences are for college, career, and self-respect, where higher status tends to entail greater perceived costs.

Grade in school was significantly related to reformatory, parental concern, college, reputation with teachers, reputation with other teenagers, and self-respect. Again, the relationships were extremely weak (-.08 to -.14). Overall, there was a slight tendency for older youth to be less concerned about the costs of labeling than younger students.

Minority status was significantly related to worries about being hurt by police, being sent to a reformatory, and being put on probation. However, again, the relationships are slight (-.03 to -.06) and contrary to what many people suspect. Anglos were most concerned, followed by Chicanos and subjects in the other racial or ethnic categories.

By far the most impressive group differences in the distribution of perceived costs involved gender (see Table 2). Females were significantly more concerned about every possible consequence of labeling than males, and the relationships were much more impressive than for other background variables. Gamma coefficients ranged from

Table 2: Perceived Costs of Labeling by Gender, 1974-1975

Perceived Costs:	High	MH	M	ML	Low	χ^2 (p≤)	√
	(In Percentages)						
Police Hurt							
Male	2	5	7	39	47	.0000	−.14
Female	4	8	5	44	39		
Reformatory							
Male	16	33	14	22	16	.0000	−.15
Female	22	35	13	20	10		
Probation							
Male	9	35	16	25	14	.0000	−.16
Female	14	39	15	22	9		
Parents Upset							
Male	63	24	5	4	4	.0000	−.37
Female	80	14	2	2	2		
Jeopardize College							
Male	38	24	9	17	12	.0000	−.17
Female	49	21	8	14	8		
Jeopardize Career							
Male	49	30	7	10	5	.0000	−.22
Female	60	27	4	5	3		
Rep with Kids							
Male	10	17	12	37	24	.0000	−.20
Female	19	22	13	26	21		
Rep with Teachers							
Male	13	22	14	28	23	.0000	−.23
Female	22	27	15	20	16		
Self-Respect							
Male	28	25	19	13	15	.0000	−.33
Female	47	25	14	8	7		

−.14 to −.37. Two of the most impressive differences involved parental reaction and self-respect. Eighty percent of the females felt that their parents would definitely be upset, as compared to 63% of the males. Forty-seven percent indicated they definitely might think badly of themselves as compared to 28% of the males. These findings are definitely consistent with views of sexual socialization as well as recent research on the sex differences in delinquency (Jensen and Eve, 1976).

The overall findings concerning the distribution of perceived costs among subgroups are quite consistent with findings concerning the distribution of self-reported delinquency. Self-report studies of delinquency find slight differences in delinquency rates by parental social status (Gold and Williams, 1972; Hirschi, 1969; Empey and Erickson, 1966), age (Hirschi, 1969), and minority status (Gold, (1970:79-81; Hirschi, 1969:75-81), but sizable differences by gender (Gold, 1970; Hindelang, 1971; Jensen and Eve, 1976) and our own data on self-reported delinquency show similar patterns. Of these four background variables gender is most strongly and consistently related to self-reported delinquency. Thus, at an aggregate level group variations in perceived costs tend to coincide with similar group variations in delinquency rates.

Delinquency and Perceived Costs

In Table 3 we have summarized the associations between each perceived cost and seven offense categories by gender. Out of 126 tests (seven offenses, nine costs x gender) there were only 17 that failed to achieve statistical significance at the .05 level. Moreover, those 17 were not randomly distributed. Nine involved perceived formal ramifications and seven involved concern over parental reaction. Of the seven involving parental reaction, six are found in the male sample.

Considering measures of association it appears that potential informal costs are more strongly related to delinquency than formal costs (especially among females). The strongest associations tend to involve concern for one's own self-respect followed by concern for other teenager's reactions. For girls, the weakest associations involve fear of being sent to a reformatory, being put on probation, or hurt by the police. For boys, the weakest associations involve concern for parental reaction, followed by reformatory, probation, and being hurt by the police.

Not only are some costs uniquely relevant to females but it appears that costs tend to be more strongly related to delinquency among them as well. Considering concerns other than parental reaction, 50 of 56 associations (seven offenses x eight costs) are stronger among females than males. Of the six exceptions, four involve reformatory,

Table 3: Gamma Coefficients Relating Perceived Costs to Delinquent Offenses by Gender

Offense Category	Minor Property	Major Property	Personal Violence	Vandalism-Auto Theft	Drugs	Drinking	Status
Police Hurt							
Male	−.15*	−.12*	−.13*	−.13*	−.10	−.16*	−.10
Female	−.17*	−.12*	−.16*	−.16*	−.12	−.14*	−.10
Reformatory							
Male	−.09*	−.15*	−.07*	−.07	−.21*	−.14*	−.14*
Female	−.13*	−.06	−.11*	−.11*	−.20*	−.14*	−.19*
Probation							
Male	−.04	−.17*	−.08*	−.10	−.15*	−.07*	−.10*
Female	−.13*	−.27*	−.16*	−.15	−.22*	−.13*	−.15*
Parents Upset							
Male	−.06	−.13	−.04*	−.03	−.18*	−.08	−.09
Female	−.28*	−.38*	−.28*	−.26*	−.35*	−.21	−.27*
Jeopardize College							
Male	−.19*	−.19*	−.15*	−.12*	−.28*	−.22*	−.22*
Female	−.32*	.32*	−.28*	−.33*	−.34*	−.29*	−.29*
Jeopardize Career							
Male	−.18*	−.16*	−.07	−.12*	−.22*	−.15*	−.17*
Female	−.26*	−.32*	−.30*	−.26*	−.29*	−.18*	−.20*
Rep with Kids							
Male	−.17*	−.24*	−.11*	−.17*	−.33*	−.32*	−.27*
Female	−.34*	−.34*	−.31*	−.32*	−.41*	−.34*	−.36*
Rep with Teachers							
Male	−.16*	−.20*	−.11*	−.16*	−.34*	−.30*	−.29*
Female	−.30*	−.28*	−.28*	−.27*	−.33*	−.26*	−.32*
Self Respect							
Male	−.23*	−.30*	−.13*	−.20*	−.35*	−.32*	−.28*
Female	−.37*	−.50*	−.40*	−.40*	−.49*	−.37*	−.41*

*Chi-square test statistic significant at the .05 level.

probation, and being hurt by the police. The other two exceptions involve concern for teacher reaction. Overall, then, females are more likely to worry about the consequences of apprehension than males, especially for informal sanctions, and such concerns tend to make a greater difference as well. It may be that delinquency among males is more a product of situational pressures and pulls, while female delinquency is more sensitive to socially structured beliefs about costs and consequences of deviant behavior.

SUMMARY AND IMPLICATIONS

Several observations have been suggested by the data summarized above. First, the major perceived consequences of labeling for adolescents are the ramifications for their self-image, their future, and significant others and not the possibility of a reformatory sentence, probation, or harm from the police. Moreover, the order and magnitude of their concerns is fairly stable over time and from one community to another.

On the other hand, there was a tendency for perceived costs to be positively associated with social status and negatively associated with age and minority status. The most striking variations were by gender, where all perceived costs were significantly higher for females. Finally, the perceived consequences of labeling for an adolescent's self-image and future and the perceived reactions of significant others are most strongly associated with delinquency, with stronger associations for females than males.

The findings have definite implications for current criminological perspectives. With regard to labeling theory it appears that those subjects who attribute stigmatic consequences to official labels are least likely to engage in behavior which is liable to labeling. Those most likely to deviate are those for whom official labeling may be socially meaningless. Thus, those most likely to be labeled may be the least likely to be affected by labeling. There is already some support for this interpretation in that studies (Jensen, 1972; Ageton and Elliott, 1974) have presented evidence suggesting that labeling is more consequential for the self-images of whites than blacks; two studies (Jensen and Jones, 1976; Harris, 1976) have suggested that prisonization processes may be more characteristic of whites as well. To understand the variable consequences of labeling requires an understanding of the social meaning of sanctions.

The data also have implications for progress in the specification of criminological theory in general. Advances in the hard sciences have involved the specification of "inertial frames" of reference, that is, those circumstances of time and space under which a set of equations applies. While there are variables which may correlate with delinquency across a broad spectrum of social or demographic groups there are others which may be uniquely relevant to select groups. Perceived costs of labeling are relevant to the delinquent activity of both males and females, but the importance of some institutional control mechanisms is variable by gender. We have shown elsewhere that religious institutions are more consequential for adolescent behavior in certain subgroups or settings than others (Jensen and Erickson, 1977). Thus, the study of the social meaning of sanctions should concertedly move toward the specification of the differential relevance of different institutional control mechanisms over time and social space. Our research should provide encouragement to those contemplating such work.

REFERENCES

AKERS, R. L. (1973). Deviant behavior: A social learning approach. Belmont, Calif.: Wadsworth.

AGETON, S. and ELLIOTT, D. S. (1974). "The effects of legal processing on delinquent orientations." Social Problems 22:87-100.

BAILEY, W. C. and LOTT, R. P. (1967). "Crime, punishment and personality: An examination of the deterrence question." Journal of Criminal Law and Criminology 67:99-109.

BAILEY, W. C. and SMITH, R. W. (1972). "Punishment: Its severity and certainty." Journal of Criminal Law and Criminology 63:530-539.

BALL-ROKEACH, S. J. (1973). "Values and violence: A test of the subculture of violence thesis." American Sociological Review 38:736-749.

BRIAR, S. and PILIAVIN, I. (1965). "Delinquency, situational inducements and commitments to conformity." Social Problems 8:35-45.

BURGESS, R. and AKERS, R. L. (1966). "A differential association-reinforcement theory of criminal behavior." Social Problems 17:128-147.

BURKETT, S. R. and WHITE, M. (1974). "Hellfire and delinquency: Another look." Journal for the Scientific Study of Religion 13:455.

CLARK, J. P. and WENNINGER, E. P. (1962). "Socio-economic class and area as correlates of illegal behavior among juveniles." American Sociological Review 27:826-834.

CLOWARD, R. A. and OHLIN, L. E. (1960). Delinquency and opportunity. New York: Free Press.

COHEN, A. K. (1955). Delinquent boys. New York: Free Press.

CONKLIN, J. E. (1975). The impact of crime. New York: Macmillan.

EHRLICH, I. (1972). "The deterrent effect of criminal law enforcement." Journal of Legal Studies 1:259-276.

EMPEY, L. T. and ERICKSON, M. L. (1966). "Hidden delinquency and social status." Social Forces 44 (June):546-554.

ERICKSON, M. L. and GIBBS, J. P. (1973). "The deterrence question: Some alternative methods of analysis." Social Science Quarterly 54:534-551.

GEERKEN, M. R. and GOVE, W. R. (1975). "Deterrence: Some theoretical considerations." Law and Society Review 9:497-513.

GIBBS, J. P. (1968). "Crime, punishment and deterrence." Social Science Quarterly 48:515-530.

GOLD, M. (1970). Delinquent behavior in an American city. Belmont, Calif.: Brooks/Cole.

GRASMICK, H. G. and MILLIGAN, H., Jr. (1976). "Deterrence theory approach to socioeconomic demographic correlates of crime." Social Science Quarterly 57 (December):608-617.

GRAY, L. N. and MARTIN, J. D. (1969). "Punishment and deterrence: Another analysis." Social Science Quarterly 50:389-295.

HARRIS, A. R. (1976). "Race, commitment to deviance and spoiled identity." American Sociological Review 41:432-442.

HENSHEL, R. and SILVERMAN, R. (1975). Perception in criminology. New York: Columbia University Press.

HINDELANG, M. J. (1971). "Age, sex and the versatility of delinquency involvements." Social Problems 18 (Spring):522-535.

——— (1973). "Causes of delinquency: A partial replication and extension." Social Problems 21:471-487.

HIRSCHI, T. (1969). Causes of delinquency. Berkeley: University of California Press.

JENSEN, G. F. (1969). "Crime doesn't pay: Correlates of a shared misunderstanding." Social Problems 17:189-201.

——— (1972). "Delinquency and adolescent self-conceptions: A study of the personal relevance of infraction." Social Problems 20:84-103.

——— and ERICKSON, M. L. (1977). "The religious factor and delinquency: Another look at the hellfire hypothesis." Paper presented at the 1977 convention of the Pacific Sociological Association, Sacramento.

JENSEN, G. F. and EVE, R. (1976). "Sex differences in delinquency: A test of popular sociological explanations." Criminology 3:427-448.

JENSEN, G. F. and JONES, D. (1976). "Perspectives on inmate culture: A study of women in prison." Social Forces 54:590-603.

JENSEN, G. F., ERICKSON, M. L. and GIBBS, J. P. (1978). "Perceived risk of punishment and self-reported delinquency." Forthcoming in Social Forces.

KRAUT, R. E. (1976). "Deterrent and definitional influences on shoplifting." Social Problems 23 (February):358-368.

LOGAN, C. H. (1972). "General deterrent effects of imprisonment." Social Forces 51:64-73.

MAHONEY, A. R. (1974). "The effect of labeling upon youths in the juvenile justice system: A review of evidence." Law and Society 8:583-614.

MERTON, R. K. (1957). Social theory and social structure. New York: Free Press.

MILLER, W. B. (1958). "Lower class culture as a generating milieu of gang delinquency." Journal of Social Issues 14:5-19.

NYE, F. I. (1958). Family relationships and delinquent behavior. New York: John Wiley.

PILIAVIN, I. M., VADUM, A. C., and ALLYN, J. (1969). "Delinquency, personal costs and parental treatment: A test of a reward-cost model of juvenile criminality." Journal of Criminal Law, Criminology and Police Science 60:165-172.

POLK, K. (1974). "Teenage delinquency in small town America." Research Report-5, National Institute of Mental Health: Center for Studies of Crime and Delinquency.

ROSSI, P. H., WAITE, E., BOSE, C. E., and BERK, R. E. (1974). "The seriousness of crimes: Normative structure and individual differences." American Sociological Review 39:224-237.

SILBERMAN, M. (1976). "Toward a theory of criminal deterrence." American Sociological Review 41:442-461.

SUTHERLAND, E. H. and CRESSEY, D. R. (1974). Criminology. Philadelphia: J. P. Lippincott.

TEEVAN, J. J. (1975). "Perceptions of punishment: Current research." Pp. 146-154 in R. L. Henshel and R. A. Silverman (eds.), Perception in criminology. New York: Columbia University Press.

THORSELL, B. A. and KLEMKE, L. W. (1972). "The labelling process: Reinforcement and deterrent." Law and Society Review (February):393-404.

TITTLE, C. R. (1969). "Crime rates and legal sanctions." Social Problems 16:405-423.

——— (1975). "Deterrents or labelling." Social Forces 53:399-410.

——— and LOGAN, C. H. (1973). "Sanctions and deviance: Evidence and remaining questions." Law and Society Review 7:371-392.

TOBY, J. (1957). "Social disorganization and stake in conformity: Complementary factors in the predatory behavior of hoodlums." Journal of Criminal law, Criminology and Police Science 48:12-17.

——— (1964). "Is punishment necessary?" Journal of Criminal Law, Criminology and Police Science 55:332-337.

TULLOCK, G. (1974). "Does punishment deter crime?" Public Interest 36:103-111.

VAN ES, J. C., and BROWN, J. E. (1974). "The rural-urban variable once more: Some individual level observations." Rural Sociology 39:373-385.

ZIMRING, F. E. and HAWKINS, G. (1973). Deterrence: The legal threat in crime control. Chicago: University of Chicago Press.

Pat Lauderdale
University of Minnesota

Harold Grasmick
University of Oklahoma

John P. Clark
University of Minnesota

9

CORPORATE ENVIRONMENTS, CORPORATE CRIME, AND DETERRENCE

Two major approaches employed in previous studies of white collar and corporate crime have provided us with important insights; however, both have a number of problems which have kept them from realizing their potential. One of the approaches is primarily atheoretical and does not lend itself to a broader understanding of corporate crime. The other basically operates from theoretical frameworks borrowed from the general fields of crime and deviance. These reworked theoretical approaches (i.e., differential association and anomie) to corporate crime possess the same disadvantages already leveled against them in the fields of deviance (Matza, 1969) and sociology of law (Black, 1976).[1] In addition, current attempts to explain corporate crime as a product of the desire to maximize profits are theoretically incomplete, ignoring contextual contradictions inherent in corporate environments (including the enactment and administration of law).

AUTHORS' NOTE: We would like to thank Ron Akers, Marshall Clinard, Phil Cunnien, Mary Jane Lehnertz, Robert Meier, Jerry Parker, and Charles Reasons for their comments on this work.

We will briefly review these prior approaches, pointing out those components which appear useful to our framework, and then present an initial attempt to construct a theory of corporate crime. In an effort to resolve some of the earlier shortcomings and develop a more general, theoretical approach to corporate crime, our work will focus upon the effects of external threats on the amount and definition of corporate crime.

There are two approaches central to the study of white collar crime: (1) identifying the types of activities that fall under that rubric, emphasizing *how* the actors engage in the activities, and discussing the use of legislation and regulatory agencies that can potentially control those offenses—a social control approach; and (2) identifying the types of activities that fall under the rubric, emphasizing *why* the actors are motivated to engage in the activities, and developing broader theories of criminal behavior—a social behavioral approach.

The *social control approach* focuses upon when the offenses are more likely to be observed and prosecuted. In one of the more comprehensive efforts utilizing this approach Tiedemann (1976) describes "economic delinquency" (in the Federal Republic of Germany, Belgium, France, England, Switzerland, and the United States) in the form of cartel offenses, fraudulent procurements of grants, computer crime, insurance fraud, fictitious or bogus firms, faking of balance sheets, and frauds concerning corporate capital.

This approach has been heuristic in a number of areas. *First,* this typological, descriptive approach has noted some of the different processes involved in white collar crime. For example, in the area of importation there are a variety of opportunities for engaging in fraudulent activities. A product with a third-world country "trademark" may be falsely retailed as a product from Europe or the United States with a mark-up in price of at least three to four times the original. Other examples are the use of dummy directors—important government officials, university professors and similar high-status actors—in corporations that are "set" for bankruptcy, and the seemingly endless variety of methods used in the commission of computer offenses. Although most of these types of crime are not new, the methods and processes of interaction constantly change; consequently, we are afforded some insight into part of the *infrastructure* of white collar crime (Gardiner, 1967; Nader, 1969; and Sale, 1977). *Second,* the approach reveals the difficulties in detecting the crime as well as the variation in the reporting of the offenses (Posner, 1970). For example, in many of the Western European countries (France, Belgium, Luxembourg, Spain, and Italy) and the United States it is extremely difficult to prove that a corporation intended to obtain an excessive profit or that a monopoly is actually being employed. In addition, frauds are rarely made public by banks or other loan-granting institutions. Revocation clauses in civil law and a system of penal interest charges make the supposed legal safeguards virtually useless (Tiedemann, 1976). *Third,* the approach has presented additional data on the relative ineffectiveness of the legal control structure. For example, Tiedemann reports that prior to 1976 the Cartel Office of the Federal Republic of Germany conducted 811 proceedings for suspected abuses of dominant market position. The result has been four sentences—none of which are final. Furthermore, small businesses in West Germany were investigated on the average of only once every 100 years and were not really included in the regulatory search.

The *social behavioral approach,* although concerned with similar offenses, primarily focuses upon why people engage in those activities and the impact of white collar crime upon larger institutional arenas. In developing a theory of why people engage in white collar crime, Sutherland's analysis still dominates most of the field. He concluded that the ideal businessman and the professional thief are strikingly similar. The businessman's violations of law are not "identical and haphazard, but they have definite policies of restraint of trade, of unfair labor prac-

tices, of fraud and misrepresentation" (1956:96). Furthermore, Sutherland stressed that the techniques of white
collar crime are learned within the context of differential
association and social disorganization, and therefore are
not the result of personal or social pathologies. Extensions
of this second approach have revealed the implications
of equating the lower- and upper-class phenomena of
crime. That is, white collar crime (like lower-class crime)
is not a result of poverty, and its occurrence indicates
fundamental changes in institutional life (these changes
include the appearance of new definitions of crime, as in
consumer fraud—Geis and Meier, 1977—as well as the
emerging conflict over the "legitimate" span of authority
in the struggle to define certain activities as criminal).[2]

This second approach, which attempts to operate from a
broad theory of criminal behavior, has been particularly
useful in providing research on the amount of corporate
crime, the number of crimes which are prosecuted, suggestions as to why there are so few prosecutions, and an
interrelated set of ideas that help to explain why people
engage in the offenses. *First,* the research on the amount
of corporate crime has complemented the discoveries by
the people working from the typological, descriptive approach. The seminal work by Sutherland (1956) revealed
that every one of the 70 largest corporations in the United
States had an adverse decision; the average number of
decisions was 14.0; 90% of the corporations could be considered habitual offenders; and 98% were recidivists. Further research has indicated the relatively large extent of
flagrantly criminal organizations (Cressey, 1972) and the
propensity of corporations to engage in routinely illegal
activities when confronted with the problem of reaching
their profit goal (Bensman and Gerver, 1973). This stream
of research helps establish a more robust data base in
conjunction with the social control approach.

Second, this approach has documented the infrequent
number of investigations and prosecutions in the white
collar crime area, as well as providing an emphasis on

theoretical suggestions for the lack of such activity. For example, the relatively low number of investigations and prosecutions can be partially attributed to (1) the _"conventional" bias in criminological work_ (i.e., social control agencies appear to spend the majority of their energy attempting to apprehend and isolate the lower-class criminal); (2) the _low visibility of white collar crime;_ (3) the _difficulties in locating "concrete" victims;_ (4) the _seemingly marginal deterrent effect of convictions;_ (5) _the fear of reprisal by the powerful corporations_ (including powerful individuals); (6) _the low probability of local prosecutors' diverting resources into the scope of investigation required for successful legal action;_ and especially (7) _the ability of powerful corporations to control or resist the definitions of criminal or criminal activities._

Third, the approach affords an initial theoretical framework. For example, Sutherland maintains that white collar crime is learned in direct or indirect association with those already engaged in the behavior, and "that those who learn this criminal behavior are segregated from frequent and intimate contacts with law-abiding behavior" (1940:11). He suggests that this behavior stems from social disorganization. That is, law presses in one direction and other social forces press in the opposite direction—in business, "the 'rules of the game' conflict with the legal rules"— which leads to social disorganization and subsequent crime. Another example of a guiding strategy operating from the second approach is presented by Gross (1976) when he claims that "the internal structure and setting of organizations is of such a nature as to raise the probability that the attainment of the goals of the organization will subject the organization to the risk of violating societal laws of organizational behavior" (1976:29-30). Furthermore, his analysis concludes that the individuals who act as agents for themselves and the organizations are likely to be "willing and able to carry out crime, should it seem to be required in order to enable the organization to attain its goals, to prosper or, minimally, to survive" (p. 30). His conclusion is based on what he considers a fairly unique set of characteristics of the *agents* of the organization (i.e., he finds the agents to possess a high level of "ambitiousness, shrewdness and moral flexibility").

In sum, the theoretical strategies that we have discussed help lay the foundation for a more complete understanding of the phenomena of white collar crime. However, the descriptive analysis from the social control approach illustrates that such a variety of phenomena cannot be adequately handled by the social behavioral approach. Furthermore, neither strategy provides (1) information as to when an individual or corporation will *initially* engage in white collar crime (e.g., Sutherland does not adequately explain how the differentially associated group came into existence); (2) a discussion of the alternative mechanisms that can potentially increase or decrease the volume (including variation in the definition) of white collar crime; and (3) a theoretical framework that helps explain how white collar crime can increase or decrease, independent of the actors within corporate organizations (i.e., both of the previous strategies are predominantly interested in answering the question of why *people* become white collar criminals).

While this third neglected area begs for attempts to explain part of white collar crime, independent of the actors within the corporations, it should also be particularly useful in achieving closure on the *variety* of mechanisms that alter the observed rate (and definition) of white collar crime. We hope to be able to identify the mechanism and processes that shift the corporate boundaries, move the actors (e.g., individuals, groups, or organizations) within those boundaries, and activate the persistently inattentive social control agencies.

THE ROLE OF EXTERNAL THREATS

Rather than using the rubric of "white collar" we will focus upon corporate social systems (Coleman, 1974) and the crime associated with those systems. Our choice of this particular analytical level is noticeably different from many conceptualizations of white collar crime. As an example, our argument does not pertain to the individual white collar criminal who may pursue private gains, but rather to collective organizational action through which the organization itself may benefit. Therefore, we can discuss the boundary movement mechanisms and processes at different types and levels of analysis. We will attempt to present a system of relationships relevant to both the smallest organizational level and multinational level (including factors such as complexity when they become appropriate).

There are a number of organizational and environmental conceptualizations and findings that may prove beneficial to the study of corporate crime. The work by Udy (1959) and Thompson (1967) suggests that as the dependency of the organization on the environment decreases, rationality within the organization will increase. That is, the effect of environmental statuses impinging upon organizational roles predicts that rationality will increase correspondingly to the degree that organizations insulate themselves from environmental pressures. Another relevant example comes from work that is located primarily in industrial economics. Asch and Seneca (1975) report significant differences in characteristics between collusive and noncollusive firms. The collusion-prone companies are generally less profitable and larger, usually centered in industries of low advertising intensity. Especially collusion-prone firms are unprofitable and large or diverse, and consumer goods firms in highly concentrated industries characterized by low entry barriers. While this type of information will be useful for a more general theory of corporate criminality, at the present they offer only some conditional requisites for a yet unconstructed theory. Presently, the assorted sets of empirical findings and conceptualizations do not come together in any interrelated form. Therefore, our first task is to present a preliminary theoretical framework for the study of corporate criminality.

Focusing upon the role of the organization's environment, we will consider how changes in a corporate social system's environment produce change in corporate crime. In particular, we will examine four potential external threats that reside in the environment of corporate social systems. This initial attempt to integrate work in the area of organizations with relevant research in deviance (Erikson, 1966; Lauderdale, 1976) suggests presenting the external threats as four analytically distinct types: (1) power realignment; (2) actions of regulatory agenceis and prosecutorial actors; (3) amplification of resource instability or depletion; and (4) new or increased competition.

Our argument suggests that changes in these threats influence the amount of corporate crime via three important processes: (1) by changing the *definition* of what is considered a crime through the creation or removal of criminal law; (2) by changing the rate at which criminal actions are *detected* through application of criminal law; and (3) by changing the *actions of actors* within the corporate system.

Changes in Definition and Detection

(1) Realignment of power refers to actions by presidents, governors, or similar high-status actors not generally considered part of the prosecutorial or regulatory system (the actors can, of course, be actors of "illegitimate" status that nonetheless have power similar to those of legitimate status). One of the classic examples of the increase in corporate criminality, independent of the actors within the corporate systems, is the accusation of crime by politicians attempting to gain entry into higher political positions: for example, the process that has led to the revelation of crime by a variety of state governmental organizations, or the process used by presidential administrations to stigmatize a variety of opposing corporate political parties. These examples illustrate that we *assume* most corporations are engaging in some criminal activities and resultant threats from the realignment of power only reveal that the crime does exist. This assumption does not seem to be in much danger of contradiction.

(2) The actions of regulatory agencies and prosecutorial actors is another example of the revelation of crime by corporations. The FCC, FDA, SEC, IRS and similar agencies may at times create the illusion that actors within corporate social systems are engaging in new or increased criminal activities when, in fact, it may be in actuality that the agencies have only dramatized (via prosecution, for example) regularly occurring events. That is, the regulatory **agencies produce an increase in corporate crime simply by selecting a portion of the ongoing criminal activities.** The U.S. Attorney's office and state prosecutorial actors appear to provide the same "artificial" increase in corporate crime. The ability of regulatory agencies and prosecutorial actors to either define an activity as criminal or process any particular criminal action is dependent on the relative power of the corporation under scrutiny (e.g., the ability of a corporation to use legal mechanisms, such as highly competent **lawyers, accountants, and the like, as well as illegal procedures** to mitigate the ability of the external control system).

(3) A concrete example of a third external threat to corporate systems, the amplification of resource instability or depletion, is illustrated by supposed increases in criminal activities by mining and manufacturing corporations. This form of threat can result from certain realignments of power or altering competition; however, it is typically amplified by a variety of consumer groups and "watch-dog" agencies. For example, in the United States various environmental protection groups are accusing the lumber firms of ruining natural resources. These groups have partially succeeded in convincing the public that the firms are engaging in new or increased criminality. However, in fact, the lumber industry has been engaging in virtually the same activities for a number of decades and this "resulting" increase in crime is primarily "artificial." Another threat and its consequences become apparent when a corporation has depleted most or all of its primary resources (e.g., U.S. oil and copper mining companies).

(4) New or increased competition is exemplified by emerging corporations presently shut off from the larger

market (Swartz, 1975:19). They may succeed in creating a social reality that consists of accusing other firms of patent violation, illegal promotions (including advertising), and political bribery. This form of external threat appears to be the most common *example* of an increase in corporate criminality; therefore, we will more completely discuss this activity in a later section.

Let us now turn to a discussion of the effect of external threats upon the actions of actors within the corporations— for while the threats can produce an increase or decrease in crime, independent of the actors in those systems, those threats can also increase or decrease the criminal activities of people within the corporate structure.

**Changes in Actions of Actors
Within Corporate Systems**

In discussing the effects of external threats on the actions of actors within corporate systems, we will draw heavily on the recently revived deterrence perspective in criminology. Our discussion will center on the mechanism we have called "regulatory agencies and prosecutorial actors," since this is the mechanism through which legal threats are typically made. However, we do recognize that the other three threats also influence the behavior of actors in the corporate system. Competition, for example, can produce increases in criminal behavior via patent violation, false advertising, and similar illegal activities that appear to keep corporations within the relevant market. External power realignments, or even potential realignment, may press actors within the system into further illegal activities in order to cover up past offenses.

The core hypothesis of deterrence theory is that increases in the certainty or severity of punishment for an offense lead to decreases in the rate or frequency of that offense. However, we suggest that, although an increase in the certainty/severity of punishment for crime X might lead to a decrease in the frequency of X, it often will lead to an increase in the frequency of crime Y. This will occur for one of two reasons. First, crime Y might cover up the fact that crime X has been committed by actors in the system, thereby allowing the corporate system to avoid punishment. Second, crime Y might be a functional alternative to crime X. If we assume that some corporate systems survive and profit because they commit crimes, then if a social control agent engages in some action which decreases the probability that a particular crime will be committed, that same action by the regulatory agency might increase the probability that some other crime will be committed. If a control agency increases its efforts to detect price fixing, one response of a corporate system might be to cease or limit its price-fixing activities and instead engage in false advertising, illegal bribes, or rebates to maintain a constant rate of profit. Thus, increased threat will have reduced the rate of a particular crime, but not the rate of crime in general. The major consequence of agency threats for the actions of actors in corporate systems may be to alter the substance of crime, not the amount.

If the certainty of punishment is near zero, as is the case for many of the corporate crimes we have been considering, an increase in the legally prescribed severity of punishment for that crime is not likely to reduce the rate of that crime. Obviously, severe punishments do not deter if the potential recipients realize that the probability they will be imposed is zero. Whereas many potential offenders might grossly overestimate the certainty of punishment for crimes such as burglary and robbery, corporate systems probably have relatively accurate estimates of the certainty of punishment for various corporate crimes. It seems reasonable to suggest that one primary role of corporate lawyers is to gather accurate information to assist the corporate system in making an estimate of the probability that a crime will be detected and punished.

Even if there is some probability that a punishment will be imposed, it still does not necessarily follow that an increase in the severity of the penalty will result in a decrease in the frequency of the crime. Ross (1976) has argued that a process of "neutralization of severe sanctions" operates within the legal system. He argues that among those who are responsible for detecting and punishing (police, judges, juries, and the like) there are norms about what constitutes "fair" punishment for various crimes. If the legally prescribed punishment is more severe than what is considered fair by those who must detect the crime and punish the offender, the probability that the crime will be detected or the accused found guilty (i.e., the certainty of punishment) decreases. Thus, beyond a certain point, as penalties become increasingly severe, the certainty of punishment can be expected to decrease, eventually to a point at which the crime rate actually increases. Ross's argument suggests the need for research concerning what is considered "fair" punishment for corporate crimes by those who do the detecting and punishing of corporate offenses. Such research might reveal that the legally prescribed penalties for many corporate crimes actually exceed what is considered fair by those actors in the regulatory agencies charged with detecting and punishing offenders. Thus, the regulatory agencies appear not to be very diligent in their efforts to detect offenses, and, indirectly, severe penalties may encourage law violations rather than deter them.

A recurring theme in the deterrence literature has been the mutual effects of threats of formal, legal punishment and informal sanctions contingent upon legal punishment in the social control process. Some writers (Zimring and Hawkins, 1973:174) have argued that the threat of legal punishment per se might not be the real deterrent; rather, the real deterrent in the legal process is the threat of informal punishments, especially stigmatization, contingent upon being legally punished for violating a law. In the absence of a threat of informal punishment contingent upon legal sanctions, the threat of legal punishment is not likely to be an effective deterrent. We would argue that this hypothesis holds only when the threatened legal punishment is relatively low in severity. A threatened *severe* penalty should be a deterrent even in the absence of informal sanctions contingent upon legal punishment. However, as suggested earlier, the certainty that a very severe prescribed penalty will be imposed appears extremely low. If only relatively mild legal penalties are imposed on actors in corporate systems who violate laws, then the threat of legal punishment is not likely to deter if informal negative sanctions are not contingent upon the legal punishment.

This raises the issue of group support for law violations in corporate systems. If there is little or no stigma attached to law violations by actors in corporate systems—and we suspect this is the case, both in terms of the reactions of other actors in the corporate system and perhaps also in terms of the reactions of the general public—then threats from agencies of relatively mild legal penalties will not be effective deterrents.

The argument above points to the final issue we wish to consider from the deterrence perspective. The rewards associated with law violation often are greater than the cost of the punishment. We already have argued that very severe penalties are not likely to be imposed for corporate crimes, and that mild penalties are not very effective deterrents in the absence of accompanying informal punishments. Consequently, for many corporate crimes, we suspect that the profits gained from the crime outweigh the cost of the punishment, both from the point of view of the corporate system and of the actors in the systems who have committed the crime in the interest of the corporate system. The fine for a patent violation in many cases is considerably less than the profits the corporate system earned from the violation. These may be both monetary and status rewards associated with violating the law on behalf of the system (Akers, 1977:229-230). On the surface, it seems that the only thing required to deter a violation would be to increase the severity of the legal penalty to the point where the violation was no longer profitable to the system and the actor. However, our earlier discussion of the neutralization of severe sanctions suggests that an increase in the severity of punishment might reduce the certainty of punishment to a point at which the frequency of the violation will increase.

In conclusion, we suggest that there is an inherent contradiction in the use of legal penalties to deter corporate crime. If a legal penalty is to be an effective deterrent, it must be severe enough to outweigh the profits gained from the crime. At the same time, it must not be so severe that it exceeds what is considered "fair" by the actors in the agencies responsible for detecting corporate crimes and prosecuting offenders. We suggest that for most corporate crimes it is impossible to establish a penalty which satisfies both of these criteria. On the one hand, the profits from corporate crimes often are immense, necessitating a very severe penalty if the threat of the penalty is to be a deterrent. On the other hand, actors in regulatory agencies, prosecutorial actors, and probably also the general public, do not consider extremely severe penalties (e.g., long prison sentences) to be "fair" punishments for corporate crimes. Therefore, the penalty will be either too mild to outweigh the advantages of the crime or too severe to be imposed.

ADDITIONAL ISSUES

Before moving on to specific hypotheses, a few points of clarification should be made. First, we have primarily focused upon increases in crime. The external threats can produce decreases in crime; however, we decided to concentrate on the increases because we assume that enactment of criminal law (e.g., definition of crime) and application of criminal law (e.g., volume of crime) typically stem from the threats. We do not think that decriminalization or decreases in the rate of crime usually follow the external threats; in fact, we assume that either would be a rare occasion.

Second, most of our theoretical argument has obviously grown out of empirical generalizations. Therefore, much of this work follows in the tradition of Sutherland's, although we hope to be able to present predictions and explanations that do not rely solely on his conceptualization of social organization. Also, recent empirical work (Goff and Reasons, 1978) appears to fit our analytical scheme quite well.

Third, the present argument can be extended to include internal threats. For example, new corporate officials can produce a decrease in crime by forcing organizational actors to eliminate patent violations; likewise, accountants can increase the rate of crime by revealing internal offenses to regulatory or prosecutorial agents.

Finally, we have also been attempting to sort out the different mechanisms and processes that lead to criminalization or decriminalization (i.e., changes in statutes, common law, and so forth). That is, criminalization/decriminalization can result directly from high-status actors (such as legislators, judges, and the like) or indirectly through regulatory/prosecutorial agents; the amplification of resource instability/depletion (via a variety of protest groups); or competitors (in the form of lobbyists).[3] We suggest that the *processes* involved in criminalization/decriminalization are somewhat different from those involved in implementation of criminal law; however, we suggest that the mechanisms are quite similar (Goff and Reasons, 1978). The *process* of passing a customer fraud law in Congress is dramatically different from putting handcuffs on a corporate executive, yet we maintain that the *mechanisms* which act as the catalysts for those processes are virtually the same. The *mechanisms* are basically different forms of external and internal threat impinging on the boundaries and actions of corporate social systems.[4]

TOWARD A THEORY OF CORPORATE CRIME

Our discussion of external threats which activate shifts in the boundaries between acceptable and unacceptable behavior by corporate bodies and the latter's reaction to these shifts is schematized in Figure 1. In sum, change in

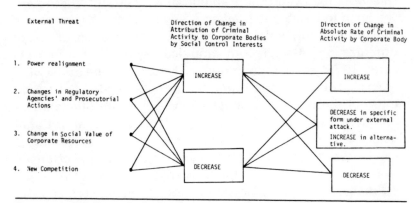

Figure 1: SUMMARY DESCRIPTIVE SCHEME OF FLUCTUATION IN COR-
PORATE CRIME RATES AS RESPONSE TO EXTERNAL THREAT

any one or a combination of any of the threats may result in an increase or decrease in the application of criminal labels to corporate actions. Additionally, this action may stimulate increases or decreases in the violative behavior by corporate bodies. The dynamics (and perhaps at times the *hydraulics*) of this situation certainly help generate the substance of corporate crime rates, both by specific offense and/or in total. Hopefully, our brief discussion above has demonstrated why it may be critical to understand the relationships among the several specific offenses which constitute the total corporate crime rate.

While our emphasis here will be upon the rate of corporate crimes, it could as well be upon their substance (definition), since our perspective specifically suggests that the content of the corporate response to external threat will reflect the substance of that threat and the range of postures the corporate body can take in response to it. For our immediate purposes, however, we propose a few hypotheses and a preliminary theoretical summary suggested by the preceding discussions.

(1) Our analysis strongly suggests that a significant proportion of the *fluctuation in corporate crime rates is a reflection of changes in constraints (threats) endogenous to corporate environments rather than changes in corporate*

action, per se. Obviously, our conceptualization of corporate *environments* is quite broad and can be emphasized by restating the hypothesis. The variation in rates is to a large extent a result of threats exogenous to corporations, rather than a result of actual behavioral changes within those bodies. One or more of the external factors can stimulate the application of criminal definitions specifically to corporate actions or, oppositely, can neutralize that process. Further, as with the informal criminalization or decriminalization of categories of individuals (e.g., "black dudes," "slum kids," "hippies," and "pot smokers"), categories of corporate bodies can through similar mechanisms be labeled in regard to their criminal propensities (e.g., "the oil companies," "used-car dealers," "nursing homes," and "advertising agencies"; see Cressey, 1973, for some empirical analysis based on "types" of corporate structures.) Put differently, environmental threats will likely impinge similarly upon corporate bodies with similar corporate characteristics. As with traditional criminal individuals and organizations, it is intellectually stimulating to consider the consequences of such a "self-validating" process. For example, the reaction to nursing home abuses or charges to Medicaid and Medicare generated a variety of greater constraints on such homes as a category, which has resulted in a flurry of additional scandals coming to the public view. At the present time there is a relatively elaborate system of controls on nursing homes and a widespread public distrust of their social value. What has been the impact of this situation on the public, on nursing home service, on nursing home "crime rates," on violative behavior? In an era of ever-increasing regulation, it is difficult to find an example of the reverse process, although the manner in which pollution from lower-grade fuels is being increasingly winked at as a concession to the energy crisis might be an area for exploration.

(2) A second working hypothesis emerging from our former comments suggests *there are only weak (insignificant?) relationships among the four external threats that*

produce changes in corporate crime rates. Tests of this hypothesis will help specify the relationships among the four environmental features which affect corporate crime rates. Taking several instances of recent rate changes in crime by organizations (nursing homes and oil industries, for example), a persistent pattern of association across these external factors is not discernible. Empirically grounded models of causation or social control under such circumstances are difficult to construct. For example, forces which generate the realignment of power at the state or national level probably are not necessarily related to the state of competition among corporations in industry sectors, although national power alignments may be at times related to the activity of regulatory agencies. With the sketchy data available now in regard to the major oil companies vis à vis their external threats, it is virtually impossible to build direct and reasonable lines of association across these factors. That is, the realignment of national powers in the environments of oil companies and their resultant indulgence in "illegal" behavior, on the surface, at least, appears to be unrelated to the condition of competition, resource instability, and regulatory assertiveness.

In fact, in attempting to draw out such relationships, one becomes inescapably aware of the *active* role corporate bodies play in helping to shape the effect external threats have upon their actions. We do not view it as a contradiction of our first general hypothesis to observe that although **corporations do not totally control the effect of external threats upon their existence, to a great extent they can** thwart, divert, or convert the thrust of the external threat to reduce its potential impact. Germane to our second hypothesis, one strategy of corporate bodies appears to be to prevent the homogenization of external threats. The goal may be to diffuse their combined effects, to the point of setting threat against threat. An example of the latter is for a corporation to neutralize both a threatening power realignment and a potentially troublesome regulatory agency by infiltrating the latter and setting it against the former, or at least controlling the agency.

Recognizing that corporate body reaction is an intervening force between an external threat and its potential consequences to the organization internally suggests the third and final general hypothesis.

(3) We suggest that external threats not only produce reinterpretations of ongoing corporate action (the substance of Hypothesis 1), but *typically also stimulate reactions by corporate actors which increase their involvement in corporate crime.* It is likely, therefore (if this relationship is empirically sustained), that shifting external definitions toward including more corporate actions under the criminal label will be compounded by increased illegal behavior on the part of corporate actors. Nonetheless, under circumstances where the external threat is perceived as overwhelming, or where the organization stands ultimately to gain, or where corporate systems are singularly committed over all else to the legal issue reflected in the regulation, external threats to the corporate body will likely elicit compliance (or at least not active resistance) from internal actors. We are impressed, however, with the rarity of the above conditions. We think it is a common occurrence to have relatively weak regulations, unresolute and ineffective enforcement, and the relatively high commitment by employees to their jobs and organizations rather than to broader social concerns. If this is the case, a realistic reaction of corporate actors under attack would be to defend their jobs and organization, or perhaps to implement the Clausewitzian maxim ("A strong defense is a strong offense") and do what must be done to counter the threat (including "cover-ups" or alternative violative behavior).

Our theoretical position is, then:

(1) The range of action by corporate bodies may be threatened by forces in their organizational environment (e.g., societal power shifts, changes in regulatory and prosecution agency assertiveness, amplification of resource instability or depletion, and varying competition).

(2) A significant amount of the fluctuation in corporate crime rates is a reflection of changes in constraints (threats) endogenous to corporate environment rather than changes in corporate action, per se.

(3) The corporate organization is capable of actively engaging the external threats and modifying their potential consequences which, under the conditions we have specified, typically result in either an increase or decrease in the corporation organization's crime rate.

(4) Given the situation of relatively high commitment to occupations and organizations, external threats to corporate bodies typically result in an increase in their illegal behavior as part of their defense against outside intrusions.

(5) Finally, two other related reactions to the threats are possible, namely a decrease in the specific offense rate of crime X but an increase in the offense rate of a similar crime Y (with an algebraic effect on the total offense rate) or, following from the conditions discussed after the third hypothesis, an absolute decrease in violative action.

NOTES

1. One of the primary problems with previous approaches is that they have operated from a fairly restricted level of analysis. For example, the perspective that suggests that individuals or corporations resort to criminal activities because they do not have the legitimate means to their goals does not explain the fact that some individuals and corporations who have the legitimate means still engage in criminal activities. Additionally, the approach fails to account for those corporations that choose to fail rather than resort to illegal activities. We think a partial solution to this type of problem is less reliance on motivational explanations and an integrated effort to work from different levels of abstraction (Lauderdale, 1976:660-663).

2. We think it is important to reiterate this part of Sutherland's work since a number of recent theorists in the social sciences have maintained that the study of white collar crime is relatively unimportant (see Wheeler, 1976, for a penetrating analysis of this situation).

3. Balbus (1977) presents a more abstract analysis of this process. His focus upon the nature of political criminalization in the liberal state illustrates the potential of the dialectical method in this area.

4. The external threats are not necessarily mutually exclusive mechanisms. For example, there may be a link between the threat of regulatory agencies and amplification of resource depletion in the varied actions of national corporations that change to multinational corporate structures. The corporations may make the move to escape regulatory controls or, at least, to lessen the number and level of

regulations. On the other hand, the corporations may be responding primarily to the resource dimensions. The new multinational position allows them to obtain the benefits of lower rates of pay to employees, cheaper materials, and similar processes that lead to gradual depletion of developing countries' resources. We simply presented the threats separately in order to illustrate their independent effects on the definition and volume of crime.

REFERENCES

AKERS, R.L. (1977). Deviant behavior: A social learning approach. Belmont, Calif.: Wadsworth.
ASCH, P. and SENECA, J.J. (1975). "Characteristics of collusive firms." Journal of Industrial Economics 23 (March):223-237.
BALBUS, I.D. (1977). "The dialectics of legal repression." New Brunswick, N.J.: Transaction.
BENSMAN, J. and GERVER, I. (1973). "Crime and punishment in the factory: The function of deviancy in maintaining the social system." American Sociological Review 28:588-598.
BLACK, D. (1976). The behavior of law. New York: Academic Press.
COLEMAN, J. S. (1974). Power and the structure of society. Philadelphia: University of Pennsylvania Press.
CRESSEY, D.R. (1972). Other people's money. Glencoe, Ill.: Free Press.
——— (1973). "Restraint of trade, recidivism and delinquent neighborhoods." In J.F. Short (ed.), Delinquency, Crime and Society. Chicago: University of Chicago Press.
ERIKSON, K.T. (1966). Wayward puritans. New York: John Wiley.
GARDINER, J. (1967). "The politics of corruption in an American city." Report to the President's Commission on Law Enforcement and Administration of Justice, Organized Crime Task Force, Washington, D.C. 67-76.
GEIS, G. and MEIER, R.F. (1977). White-collar crime. New York: Free Press.
GOFF, C.H. and REASONS, C. (1978). Corporate crime in Canada. Englewood Cliffs, N.J.: Prentice-Hall.
GROSS, E. (1976). "Organizational crime: A theoretical perspective." Department of Sociology, University of Washington, Seattle. (unpublished)
HAGE, J. (1972). Techniques and problems of theory construction in sociology. New York: John Wiley.
KATZ, J. (1977). "Cover-up and collective integrity: On the natural antagonism of authority internal and external to organizations." Social Problems 25 (October):3-17.
LAUDERDALE, P. (1976). "Deviance and moral boundaries." American Sociological Review 41: 660-676.
MATZA, D. (1969). Becoming deviant. Englewood Cliffs, N.J.: Prentice-Hall.
NADER, R. (1969). "Business crime." Pp. 138-140 in D. Sanford (ed.), Hot war on the consumer. New York: Pitman.
POSNER, R.A. (1970). "A statistical study of antitrust enforcement." Journal of Law and Economics 13 (October): 365-419.
ROSS, H. L. (1976). "The neutralization of severe penalties: Some traffic law studies." Law and Society Review 10 (Spring):403-413.

SALE, K. (1977). "The world behind Watergate." Pp. 240-252 in G. Geis and R. Meier (eds.), White-Collar Crime. New York: Free Press.

SUTHERLAND, E. H. (1940). "White-collar criminality." American Sociological Review 5 (February): 1-12.

——— (1956). "Crime of corporations." Pp. 78-96 in A. Cohen, A. Lindesmith, and K. Schuessler (eds.), The Sutherland papers. Bloomington: Indiana University Press.

SWARTZ, J. (1975). "Silent killers at work." Crime and Social Justice 3 (Summer): 15-20.

TIEDEMANN, K. (1976). "Phenomenology of economic crime." Report presented to the Twelfth Conference of Directors of Criminological Research Institutes, Council of Europe, Strasbourg (August).

THOMPSON, J. D. (1967). Organizations in action. New York: McGraw-Hill.

UDY, S. H. (1959). Organization of work: A comparative analysis of production among non-industrial peoples. New Haven, Conn.: Human Relations Area Files Press.

WHEELER, S. (1976). "Trends and problems in the sociological study of crime." Social Problems 23 (June): 525-534.

ZIMRING, F. and HAWKINS, G. (1973). Deterrence: The legal threat in crime control. Chicago: University of Chicago Press.

ABOUT THE AUTHORS

MARVIN D. KROHN is Assistant Professor of Sociology at the University of Iowa. His research interests include cross-national comparisons of crime, adolescent substance use, and legal socialization.

RONALD L. AKERS is Professor and Chairman of the Department of Sociology at the University of Iowa. He has research interests in criminology, sociology of the law, and deviance. He is author of *Deviant Behavior: A Social Learning Approach,* and co-editor of *Law and Control in Society* and *Crime Prevention and Social Control.*

RICHARD A. BALL is Professor of Sociology at West Virginia University. His current interests include research on rural delinquency and a continuation of his theoretical work in dialectical and general systems theory. He has recently published articles in both of these areas.

PATRICIA L. BRANTINGHAM is Assistant Professor in the Department of Criminal Justice at Simon Fraser University. Her research interests include crime prevention through environment design, court systems, and mathematical criminology. Currently she is co-principal investigator on a Canadian national project comparing public defenders with court appointed attorneys. She is co-author of *Geometry of Crime* (forthcoming).

PAUL J. BRANTINGHAM is Associate Professor in the Department of Criminal Justice at Simon Fraser University. His research interests include the spatial analysis of crime, the juvenile justice system, and deterrence. He is co-author of a forthcoming book entitled *Geometry of Crime* (Brantingham and Brantingham) and co-editor of *Juvenile Justice Philosophy* (Faust and Brantingham).

JOHN P. CLARK is Professor of Sociology at the University of Minnesota. His current research interests include social control organizations and organizational deviance.

RAND D. CONGER is Assistant Professor of Sociology at the University of Georgia. He is currently interested in family violence and continuing his work in empirically testing social learning theory and applying it to the operation of the criminal justice system. He has combined these two interests in his current work on intervention programs to prevent family violence employing social learning techniques. He is co-author of a forthcoming article in *Child Development* on family interaction in abusive, neglectful, and normal families.

MAYNARD L. ERICKSON is Professor of Sociology at the University of Arizona. He is currently engaged in two major research projects: an evaluation of diversion from the criminal justice system and the public's knowledge and perception of the law, crime, and delinquency.

RONALD A. FARRELL is Professor of Sociology at the State University of New York at Albany. He is author of *Inequality and the Law, The Substance of Social Deviance* and co-editor of *Social Deviance.* His current research interest is in the role of criminal conceptions in the legal process.

159

JOHN F. GALLIHER is Professor of Sociology at the University of Missouri. He is currently continuing his research on the political, cultural, and social origins of the written criminal code and on the ethics and politics of social science research in American sociology. Among his recent publications are a 1974 *Law and Society Review* article investigating the origins of the Nebraska marijuana law and a 1977 *Social Problems* article critiquing the research on the formation of the Marijuana Tax Act.

HAROLD GRASMICK is Assistant Professor of Sociology at the University of Oklahoma. His research interests include deterrence and the effects of social change. He has a forthcoming article in *Rural Sociology* on cultural lag and is currently working on a research project investigating the deterrence doctrine.

RUTH ELLEN GRIMES is a Ph.D. candidate in the Department of Sociology, University of Toronto. Her dissertation research is a historical case analysis of rape.

JEFFREY M. HYMAN received his Ph.D. from Bowling Green State University. His research interests include prisonization, deterrence, and public attitudes toward police effectiveness. He is co-author of an article on public attitudes toward police effectiveness which appeared in *Police Science Quarterly*.

GARY F. JENSEN is Associate Professor of Sociology at the University of Arizona. He is currently working on a research project investigating the social meaning of sanctions and is interested in extending social control theory. Among his recent publications are articles on the perceived risk of punishment and the religious factor in delinquency.

PAT LAUDERDALE is Assistant Professor of Sociology at the University of Minnesota. He is currently interested in political deviance.

HAROLD E. PEPINSKY is Associate Professor of Forensic Studies and East Asian Languages and Cultures at Indiana University, Bloomington. Trained in Chinese language and literature, law, and sociology, he is the author of *Crime and Conflict: A Study of Law and Society* (Academic Press, 1976), and of numerous articles and chapters on criminal justice decision-making, crime measurement, and comparative macroanalyses of crime control. Another book by him, a criminology text focusing on crime control strategies, is in preparation with Oxford University Press.

VICTORIA SWIGERT is Assistant Professor of Sociology at Holy Cross College. She is currently interested in the role of criminal conceptions in the legal process. She is co-author of *Murder, Inequality and the Law* and *The Substance of Social Deviance* as well as co-editor of *Social Deviance*.

CHARLES W. THOMAS is Professor of Sociology at Bowling Green State University. His current research interests are public attitudes toward capital punishment, labeling theory, and employee crime. He has forthcoming articles on capital punishment *(Social Problems)* and public attitudes toward punishment *(Sociological Focus)*.

AUSTIN T. TURK is Professor of Sociology and Criminology in the Department of Sociology and Center of Criminology at the University of Toronto. His research interests include the sociology of law, deviance, and social control, and theoretical criminology. He is the author of a forthcoming book entitled *Political Criminality and Political Policing*.